SARAH BARMAK

CLOSER

NOTES FROM THE ORGASMIC FRONTIER OF FEMALE SEXUALITY

COACH HOUSE BOOKS, TORONTO

Published with the generous assistance of the Canada Council for the Arts and the Ontario Arts Council. Coach House Books also gratefully acknowledges the support of the Government of Canada and the Government of Ontario.

LIBRARY AND ARCHIVES CANADA CATALOGUING IN PUBLICATION

Barmak, Sarah, author
    Closer : notes from the orgasmic frontier of female sexuality / Sarah Barmak.

(Exploded views)
Issued in print and electronic formats.
ISBN 978-1-55245-323-0 (paperback).-

    1. Female orgasm. 2. Women--Sexual behavior. 3. Sexual excitement.
4. Sex (Psychology). 5. Sex (Biology). 6. Libido. I. Title. II. Series:
Explodedviews

HQ29.B36 2016   306.7082   C2016-902854-2

Closer is available as an ebook: ISBN 978-1-77056-439-8 (epub), ISBN 978-1-77056-440-4 (pdf), ISBN 978-1-77056-456-5 (mobi).

To Jeff

Well you see like a woman has a few things going for her, not very many but she has a few things going for her and one of them is uh, dare I mention it, a clit-clitoris and uh, whooo, a clitoris, yes. And what happens is that this old, this old clitoris of hers, it starts to thumpin. It starts to thumpin and it starts to humpin, and it starts to throbbin and it starts to sobbin, and this old !%6* %4*& %*?&:! $;//1 WHOOOOO! Well what happens is that you lie there and you get sort of helpless see, and like you get, it's kinda freeze it's kinda like a coke freeze if you know what I'm talkin about. Okay so you get this freeze and like you feel kind of helpless and you're lying there and it's like this little tiny part of you starts to scream this really really fine, exquisite, high pitched scream and it's, it's like a wire, it's kind of like a wire that leads out into the sun that you find yourself being flung along arbitrarily and you don't mind in the least, you know you just go whoo-oo, you just go up there and um, it's good sheet, yeh coming is good sheet.

– 'Georgiana,' interviewed by A.S.A. Harrison in *Twenty-Two Women Talk Frankly about Their Orgasms* (Coach House Press, 1974)

1

Fear of Pleasure

In a sex-obsessed culture, not all of us feel at home..

There was something mysterious the matter with me, something
that could not be put right like bad breath or over-looked like
pimples, and everybody knew it, and I knew it; I had known it
all along.

— Alice Munro, 'Red Dress'

The ladies trickle, slowly and tentatively, into the sex shop.
Rather than turning right through the main door toward
the sales floor's hot-pink vibrators and tattooed staff, they
keep left, climbing a narrow staircase into a little carpeted
attic. They shake rainwater off their umbrellas and find seats
in the circle of chairs, scooting around each other and
mumbling *excuse mes* and *sorrys*. They look shyly at their laps,
poke at their phones. One floor above the array of silicone
toys promising advanced pleasure to the adventurous, these
fifteen or so women aged twenty to sixty are here on a much
braver quest: to learn how to have an orgasm. For nearly all,
it will be their first one.

In contrast to the riotous main floor of Good For Her,
Toronto's sex store built for women, the quiet attic is solemn,
its lights soft. The five-hour workshop, held on a drizzly Sunday
morning in April, isn't meant for drop-ins. Participants have
planned many weeks in advance, driving in from surrounding
suburbs, leaving kids with grandparents or husbands.

The store's founder, Carlyle Jansen, stands, tall and self-
contained. 'This is probably the first time you've been around
people who understand you,' she says softly. She asks everyone
to say their name, a little about why they're here and, lastly,
to share something they have recently learned.

The room is quiet. Someone clears her throat.

'Hi, I'm Sherry. I've never had an orgasm,' begins one woman, with a mix of reluctance and relief. 'Um … and I'm learning to salsa dance.'

'Thank you, Sherry,' says Jansen.

'My name's Maya,' says a young woman (names and identifying details of participants have been changed). 'I've never had an orgasm. Growing up I never masturbated or anything. I didn't find it pleasurable. I just felt really like, why am I doing this? Anyway. And juicing's my new thing.'

Like alcoholics at an AA meeting, they each make their admission. There is Denise, who says apologetically that she's 'from the suburbs.' She laughs, then blurts out a story. 'I was sexually molested by my cousin when I was seven. Messed up, right? I only lost my virginity when I was twenty-eight. I faked it.' Tears well up in her eyes.

The women are married, divorced, single. They're all straight – except, perhaps, for one who keeps asking how she'd know if she was a lesbian. Dressed in sensible sweaters and jeans, they cross their ankles under their chairs. Most seem as though they have deliberately avoided the topic of whether they're satisfied with their sex lives until now.

'I'm forty-seven,' says a woman named Jill. 'Three weeks ago I went on OkCupid. And I made out with a bartender. I thought my vagina was dead. When I talked to this guy, my vagina started *tingling*.' Laughter ripples around the room. 'I'm like, what is that? It's never happened in my life. And it's kind of scary because I don't want –' Jill's voice cracks. 'I don't want to be addicted to this guy. I don't want him to have that kind of power.'

'You won't,' says Jansen, gently. 'It's *your* power.'

'I'm married,' says one woman. 'We have a really loving marriage now, but for a while we had a pretty bad sex life. I remember after my son was born they didn't stitch me up properly so it was very, very painful. And it didn't matter to my husband, so I had to have sex a lot …'

'I was molested by my cousin when I was about thirteen,' says a participant named Kathleen. 'I don't think I knew I had a vagina until I was an undergrad. I thought I was frigid. And I don't know if it's because of what happened to me as a child or not, but I've never been – like, I can get myself to a precipice, but I can never … right?'

'Yeah, uh-huh,' says someone.

'Like it becomes too intense, and I can't,' says another.

'Anybody feel like they get stuck on that edge, that precipice?' asks Jansen. There are muttered yeses.

'I feel it's that my body might be ready to, but I'm not,' offers one woman.

'Anybody ever have the experience, you're having sex but you're just there, you're not noticing what's going on?' asks Jansen. 'You're not feeling what's going on down there when you're in your head thinking about "Am I going to have an orgasm? Am I not? Am I wet enough? Do I look sexy?"'

'And those *noises*,' offers Jill. 'When you're self-conscious, you're like, "Oh, that sounds weird." How do you stop thinking? *How do you stop thinking?*'

'It was my birthday last week,' says a woman named Michelle. 'I'm fifty-six. I don't want to be single anymore. And I think I use this as an excuse. Because you can have relationships even though you don't have orgasms, right? But I can't. Or I've set up that block for myself, right?'

'I finally want to have a real orgasm. I think I deserve that. That's why I'm here.'

'For me there's a lot of shame wrapped up in this topic.'

'I'm excited and I'm also terrified.'

'I've spent my whole life running the other way. And I'm ready to stop doing that.'

'I signed up for this course, okay?' says Denise, wiping tears off her cheeks. 'I drove here. I'm proud of myself. This is all very scary for me.'

'Can anyone else relate?' asks Jansen. There are murmured yeses.

The women in the room don't come from especially repressive households. For the most part, they hail from Toronto, Etobicoke, Guelph – in a province governed by a lesbian premier, surely among the most progressive places in the world for girls to grow up. Some have suffered trauma and molestation, but not all. What they share is a secret. This special thing that is supposed to happen in the bodies of 'normal' women – ideally in a shower of stars and rainbows and *wow* – refuses to happen, and they don't know why. Some can't touch themselves. Some won't let anyone perform oral sex on them because they think their privates are 'weird' and 'dirty.' A couple of them have 'gotten there' – but only if their partners aren't in the room.

There is no pill they can take, no doctor they can see. The secret compounds with age: the older they get, the more some figure they should just let the whole thing go. To some, too, it feels self-indulgent to even complain about such a thing. What's an orgasm, anyway? Just a momentary *pop* that disappears as soon as it's begun. It's not a *real* problem. Yet all these busy, seemingly practical women are here.

'I am *afraid* to have an orgasm,' says Denise. She leans forward, her bangs hanging over reddened eyes. 'I'm afraid of losing control … I think I've come close, maybe. But I stop myself, because I'm *afraid*.'

'Yup. Anybody else?' asks Jansen.

Hands go up around the room.

A half-century ago, the story goes, there was a sexual revolution. Skirts got shorter, rock 'n' roll got louder and sexuality was freed from its chains. We could pinpoint the exact moment, if we like, to 1956, when Elvis Presley caused a ruckus by gyrating his pelvis on black-and-white television: his hip-thrusting was so dangerous that the cameramen on *The Ed Sullivan Show* were instructed to film him from the waist up. Or maybe the revolution really happened in the sixties, when the birth-control pill was approved in the U.S. (and eventually Canada), permanently disentangling the act of intercourse from its most common hazard – pregnancy. In theory, it freed millions of women to do the thing men had always felt free to do.

From that decade onward, human sexuality was set loose to do its freaky, funky thing. Freudian psychology and the collective hormones of young baby boomers combined to liberate sex from the repressive jail it had been held in throughout history. It was all Ursula Andress in a wet bikini on the beach and copies of *Playboy* in the dentist's office and Alfred Kinsey and Woody Allen telling us everything about which we were once, but no longer, afraid to ask.

Cut to a couple generations later, and our modern world is pure sex. Images of graphic coupling (or tripleting, or quintupling) are instantly available at the touch of a smartphone. The average music video has more high-definition close-ups of glistening, naked glutes than porn had in the seventies. Indeed, porn has become our mainstream aesthetic. Our ideal body is one that is sculpted, tanned and hairless – ready for nudity at a moment's notice, as if a tripod, some Klieg lights and a mustachioed director are always lurking around the next corner. In other words, the world couldn't get any more liberated than it already is, and if it could, one wouldn't want it to.

Reality, however, is more complicated. Although we appear liberated on the surface – our clothing, our language and our media are more explicit than ever before – many of us feel overwhelmed, struggling to make space for our individual sexuality among so many idealized images. And if the person you ask is a woman, it may not be clear what the sexual revolution did for her.

A striking number of women today have a sexual complaint. Over half report some kind of difficulty with sex, according to Britain's 2013 National Survey of Sexual Attitudes and Lifestyles, and more than one in ten are distressed about their sex life. Up to 40 percent of women aged sixteen to forty-four say they lack motivation to have sex. Dyspareunia, persistent pain during vaginal penetration, affects 8 percent of women, particularly those under thirty-five. The 2013 survey also found 16 percent of women complained of anorgasmia, the difficulty with or inability to orgasm, and 12 percent said they just don't enjoy sex. Many more women have never climaxed, or aren't sure – about 16 percent of women aged twenty-eight or younger, in fact. Amid the mainstream women's magazines spurring us on to *Bigger! Longer!* and *Multiples!*, it's an issue that must feel invisible.

Most striking is the so-called 'orgasm gap': a mere 57 percent of women aged eighteen to forty usually climax during sex with a male partner, while their partners come 95 percent of the time, according to a 2015 *Cosmopolitan* survey of over 2,300 women, conducted by Anna Breslaw and others. Keep in mind that these numbers come from cultures we think of as relatively sexually liberated – Canada, the U.S. and Great Britain.

In other words, a lot of ordinary women have a bad time in bed. But because we've avoided studying women's sexuality for so long, we don't have much of an understanding of why this is. Despite the rise of sexuality studies in the sixties and seventies and the eruption of new research on men's sexual issues following the 1998 U.S. Food and Drug Administration approval of sildenafil (Viagra) to treat erectile dysfunction, comparatively little research has been done into women's sexuality (and even less has addressed the experiences of gay and trans men and women). A 2006 search of the U.S. National Library of Medicine found it held 14,000 publications on male sexual disorders, but only 5,000 on those affecting women, according to the book *The Science of Orgasm*. That's almost three times as many studies of male sexual problems than of those experienced by women, even though many experts characterize women's sexuality as more complex.

Drug companies have been eyeing the ranks of unfulfilled women as a potential marketer's bonanza. For years, a race has been on to develop a miracle treatment for women's sexual ills – a pill, cream, injection or even surgery that could give women the ability to feel urgent desire or to have bigger, more satisfying climaxes on demand. Dissatisfaction has made some women desperate for medical solutions. Some even risk painful and dangerous procedures such as clitoral-hood surgery, where tissue is cut away to increase sensitivity, as well as to try and emulate the neat, tidy genitalia seen in porn – a designer vulva. At stake in this medical push are untold profits: annual sales of Viagra stand at around US$2 billion. Its main developer, Dr. Simon Campbell, got a knighthood in 2014 for services rendered to science and mankind.

Despite nearly two decades of searching for a 'pink Viagra,' however, drug companies have failed. Women's sexual systems have proven reluctant to being jump-started by drugs. This is partly due to the greater complexity of women's anatomical and nervous systems. But there is also the inconvenient fact that sexuality in women tends to involve our *whole selves*, not just our anatomy. How does one synthesize the intoxicating state of mind-body excitement so key to female arousal, or the feeling of safety and trust that is often essential for it? The answer is beyond the scope of pharmacology. The only medication approved so far for the treatment of low desire in women, flibanserin (brand name Addyi) in 2015, is controversial. Doctors and researchers have criticized it as ineffective – women who took it had just one more 'sexually satisfying event' per month than those on a placebo – and even dangerous, with a risk of side effects such as low blood pressure and fainting. Vancouver sex therapist David McKenzie worries the drug will result in yet higher expectations on women. '[It] puts more pressure now on women, probably from male partners, to step up to the plate,' he told the *Globe and Mail*. Alongside drugs, a cottage industry of technology to artificially turbo-charge female sexuality has sprung up in recent years, including wired Kegel exerciser gadgets women can insert in their vaginas to gather data about the tightness of their vaginal walls (*Still too loose – better do another hundred squeezes!*), and the 'G-shot,' an injection that purports to boost G-spot sensation.

Something is off about this picture. Being dysfunctional is so common that it's the new normal. If women are as likely to have some kind of complaint as they are of being 'functional,' do we need to rewrite our definition of 'functional'? What if female sexuality is not the problem – what if our idea of 'normal' is the problem?

'I demand that I climax.' In 2015, rapper Nicki Minaj made headlines when she told *Cosmopolitan* that women should demand pleasure. 'I have a friend who's never had an orgasm in her life. In her life! That hurts my heart. It's cuckoo to me.' She says she and her friends 'always have orgasm interventions where we, like, show her how to do stuff. We'll straddle each other, saying, "You gotta get on him like that and do it like this."'

She and comedian Amy Schumer must be comparing notes. 'Make sure he knows that you're entitled to an orgasm,' said Schumer in an interview with *Glamour* one month later, just one of several times she's brought female pleasure to the fore. 'I like to say it. I'll be like, "Hey, there are two people here,"' Schumer continued. 'I'll be like, "Oh my God, have you met my clit?" Don't be self-conscious.' These appearances of the clitoris in mainstream media helped get 2015 declared the 'year of the female orgasm' by news site *Mic*.

There's a reason two of the biggest female entertainers in America are speaking up about female pleasure, and it's not to shock. It's because they know ordinary women are speaking more and more like this already.

And they aren't just talking amongst themselves. Surrounded by images of sex, yet starved of concrete information, driven by a desire for alternatives to pills or superficial sex tips, women are seeking out facts, experimenting with a wider range of activities and, in the process, transforming their relationship to their sexuality. Medicalizing sexual issues can often make women feel *worse* – being labelled 'abnormal' isn't exactly a recipe for feeling sexy. This interest is propelling sales of a crop of female-focused sex guides, such as Emily Nagoski's *Come As You Are*, Ian Kerner's *She Comes First* and Allison Moon's queer- and trans-friendly *Girl Sex 101*. Diverse women – therapists, mothers, neuroscientists and orgasmic cult members – are all asking, in their own ways, whether the complexity of female sexuality is a quality worth celebrating rather than a dysfunction to be cured.

As a journalist, I wanted to look at the myriad cultural undercurrents that are challenging old beliefs about women's sexuality, even as stereotypes persist and reappear in other ways. I was curious about why female sexuality seems more on the radar now than ever – yet it often seems no closer to being well understood. I can't remember when I first encountered the idea that female sexuality was a big *mystery* – that men have simple, straightforward equipment, but women have tricky puzzles, fleshy Rubik's cubes. I seem to have always been aware of it. But I found it underscored by a popular *New York Times Magazine* psychology story in 2009, 'What Do Women Want?' that I wore out with rereading, its unsettling question – famously posed by Freud to one of his female patients – embedding itself in my head like a burr in a sweater. *What do we want?* I explored this question with women from varied backgrounds, and it became clear that they wanted to know the answer, too. They gave me clues: read this sex book, talk to this therapist, go to this meetup, take this tantra course. So I did. I gradually uncovered networks of sex-loving women answering that question for themselves in highly individual ways. This little book is the result.

Closer delves into the cutting-edge science of sex that's being done in fMRI (functional magnetic resonance imaging) machines and in labs, where we'll meet researchers striving to understand the matrix of female sexuality as a whole – the complex nerves, hormones, neurotransmitters, neural circuitry, emotions, cultural pressures and expectations that all contribute to arousal, satiety and well-being – among them a Canadian psychologist who is pioneering mindfulness meditation as a sexual treatment. We'll also explore the adventurous ways some women are redefining their sexuality, whether by attending live demonstrations of orgasm at Burning Man or seeking unconventional therapists who use sensual touch to heal trauma. Inspired by the sex-positive women's movements of the 1970s and buoyed by the current popularity of yoga and holistic health, these subcultural rustlings are slowly surfacing from underground to mainstream.

This is the art and craft of women's sexuality, as opposed to the science. It is weird, wonderful and at times bizarre. This book offers a brief tour through this juicy, exciting frontier.

I was motivated to write this book by a paradox. Sex is one of the greatest things about being alive. As science journalist Zoe Cormier writes, human sexuality is unique on the planet: biologists believe we likely experience more pleasure from the dance of mating than any other organism. For most animals, copulation is nasty, brutish and short. Humans make love for fun, self-expression and emotional closeness – and we can do it for hours. The human woman possesses a clitoris and the ability to have multiple orgasms. You'd think that for ladies, life ought to be a party. But it hasn't worked out that way.

Sex remains a polarizing topic in the Western world, and it's especially conflicted when it comes to women. Women are still shamed for expressing their sexuality, whether it's former CNN host Piers Morgan using his Twitter platform to denounce reality star Kim Kardashian for sharing her latest Instagram nude, or authorities' habit of blaming sexual assault on victims. (When a Toronto police officer told a roomful of students at York University that to protect themselves from rapists, 'women should avoid dressing like sluts,' he inadvertently sparked the worldwide SlutWalk movement in 2011, with women taking to the streets in fishnets and lingerie.) At the same time, women are pressured to be sexually attractive and orgasmic. But the omnipresence of homogeneously hyper-sexualized images in our daily lives has become far more oppressive than liberating.

In the vacuum left by an inadequate sex education that focuses more on preventing pregnancy and STDs than on pleasure, a new generation is coming of age learning about sex from a skewed source: porn, in which women go from zero to hardcore penetration in all orifices without a hint of foreplay. The app Tinder is transforming dating into a hyper-accelerated game, where men compete to hook up with as many women as possible. In a 2015 *Vanity Fair* story by Nancy Jo Sales, young women who have used the app said it seems to remove incentives for guys to try please them in bed, since they can always move on to a new match.

'What's a real orgasm like?' lamented one young woman. 'I wouldn't know.'

'It's a contest to see who cares less, and guys win a lot at caring less,' said another.

Women climax twice as often in committed relationships as they do in one-night stands, according to a study presented in 2013 by Justin R. Garcia, assistant professor of gender studies at the Kinsey Institute at Indiana University and Binghamton University. This isn't a plea for monogamous values – many women like no-strings sex as much as men. Rather, it is recognition of the fact that women are simply more likely to come if their partners care about their pleasure and participants feel comfortable communicating about what they want, which seems less common in hookups. Some men questioned in the study actually said they worried less about their partners' pleasure if the sex was casual.

'We have to conclude ... that the Western sexual revolution sucks,' declared Naomi Wolf in her provocative 2012 manifesto *Vagina: A New Biography*. 'It has not worked well enough for women.'

It's not clear that our amped-up sexual culture serves men very well, either. You won't hear this from the commercials, but about half of men who are prescribed Viagra stop the treatment, most within three months, according to a 2012 study led by psychologist Ana Carvalheira. Some men are making open declarations about kicking their porn habit because it is ruining real sex; Ran Gavrieli's 2013 TED talk, 'Why I Stopped Watching Porn,' in which he opens up about the way hardcore porn warped his fantasies, has nearly 12 million views.[1]

There may well be a kinder, gentler side to men's sexuality that is being erased in this culture. A male friend of mine has trouble climaxing unless he feels deeply comfortable with a woman, which could take months of dating – but you can bet he doesn't talk about it much in a society that rewards men for racking up one-night stands. Most intriguing of all are the young men flocking to join OneTaste, an organization that promotes 'orgasmic meditation,' or OM – a sex practice that focuses on women's pleasure. Men stay clothed and stroke women's genitals with a finger for fifteen minutes, and the encounter ends there. The practice is thought to increase connection and sensation for both partners, and it's erupting in popularity as a kind of 'slow sex' – the answer to slow food.

This book isn't arguing against pornography. It's certainly not saying men's sexuality is inherently bad or harmful, or that women are from Venus and thus have different needs than men, who are from Mars. Gender and sexual difference is not a female/male binary at all, but a wide, protean spectrum, and the word *woman* can refer equally to cisgender, intersex, genderqueer and transgender women, all representing varied shades of experience. The struggle of cis women – who identify with the gender assigned to them at birth, in contrast to transgender – to blow open and redefine sexuality on their own terms is strongest when they amplify the voices of women who are most marginalized, especially trans women. Meanwhile, teens represent an emerging freedom from gender norms the rest of the world hasn't begun to imagine; according to a 2016 study by market research firm J. Walter Thompson Intelligence, 78 percent of U.S. teens aged thirteen to twenty said gender doesn't define a person as much as it used to. If this book tends to fall back on referring to women and men as two options in a binary set, that is only to enable me to look at ways women's needs and desires specifically differ from men's differences that have been erased and vilified for thousands of years – and not, hopefully, to re-entrench them.

I titled this book *Closer* after a hard-to-describe moment that may be intimately familiar to human beings with a clitoris. It's the knotty point during sex when you realize an orgasm is just over the horizon, just within your reach. It's as if you've climbed to the top of a rollercoaster, but you're stuck in mid-air without plummeting over the edge, like a naked, sweaty Wile E. Coyote. It is a tense, often infuriating moment. You may be anxious about taking too long, about wasting your partner's time. 'I'm getting closer,' you say hopefully. The more worry builds about reaching that goal, however, the more likely it is that the orgasm will deflate and vanish. According to the 2015 *Cosmopolitan* survey, 50 percent of women know this well – they almost get there, but can't.

That may sound like a strange rationale for naming a book, and it is. But 'closer' also refers to the way we are finally, tentatively approaching deep realizations about the female body, and about the ability of sexuality to develop closeness – to yourself, your partners, your fellow humans.

I'm not writing this book as a sex guide, or to help women have bigger, longer or multiple orgasms. There are many fine and helpful books on those subjects, and it's been a distinct pleasure to read them in the course of my research. They are listed in my Works Cited and Suggested Reading at the back of this book, and I encourage readers to help themselves to the riches therein. Instead, this book is meant simply as a taste, a provocation, food for further thought. Women are reshaping their sexuality today in wild, irrepressible ways, whether through conscious pornography, group masturbation or redefining the word *orgasm* itself, and, in a world that pressures girls to fit in, this unselfconscious weirdness is a gift.

One could ask whether all this groping for ecstasy is any more than hedonistic pleasure-seeking. Is any of it relevant to the big picture of women's lives, considering wage and other inequalities – doesn't the burden of demanding work and childcare kill much of the time we have left for sex anyway? I hope to show that the search for sexual equality is integral to the greater discussion taking place about women's rights. It intersects with well-being, self-determination and consent. However, it's important to note that this short book doesn't in any way pretend to be a comprehensive look at female sexuality all over the globe in 2016; because of research constraints, it's limited to women in what we might think of as the secular

West, particularly North America. That doesn't mean women aren't finding intriguing ways to push sexual boundaries around the world, where women's rights are threatened or nonexistent[2] – just that it wouldn't be my place to pronounce on them here.

At the Good For Her workshop in Toronto, more than one woman confessed they were seized with fear when they tried to orgasm. But how could anyone be afraid of pleasure? Isn't it the opposite – *not* coming – that's supposed to be intolerable?

It's been said that for women, sex is never an isolated act. Sexuality tends to affect and be affected by the rest of life. 'Pleasure is all of you,' writes Emily Nagoski, a process that results from the interaction of stress, memory, body image, nervous system, trust and even the smells in the room. That's what makes medicating it nearly impossible. If pleasure scares us, it's a sign we may want to heed rather than plow past. It may be a feature rather than a bug. Being exquisitely vulnerable while another person is witnessing your rolled-back zombie eyes and animal grunts can feel risky. If sex is worth it, writes author Mikaya Heart, it's because 'letting go of what other people think is the single most important thing you can do to improve the quality of your life in general and your sex life in particular.'

The women at the workshop spent five difficult hours learning their anatomy, hearing that what was between their legs wasn't disgusting. They learned how to ask for what they wanted in bed, laughed and confronted deep-seated fears. The most powerful thing they learned as they listened to each other was that other women were just like them. They were normal after all.

2

A History of Forgetting

How centuries of ignorance of the female anatomy is still wreaking havoc on women's health today – and how one woman fought back.

The discovery that she is castrated is a turning-point in a girl's growth.

— Sigmund Freud, 'Femininity,' *New Introductory Lectures on Psycho-Analysis* (1933)

Vanessa lay back on her family doctor's examination table and, quickly and efficiently, began to masturbate with one hand. Her other hand was busy holding her cellphone, aiming its camera down between her legs. She checked the picture, making sure she was in frame. Her doctor was just outside the room, waiting for Vanessa to finish.

Vanessa wasn't getting herself off under the bracing lights of an exam room for kicks. She was doing it to prove to her doctor that a controversial part of her anatomy existed. She was going to provide video evidence of a woman ejaculating. That may sound unnecessary to anyone who's seen much porn, where expelling anywhere from a few drops to a full cup of liquid – or 'squirting' – during or just after an orgasm is currently one of the most in-demand fetish acts a woman can perform on camera. But despite all the squirting videos flooding the market, Vanessa's doctor had never heard of it. 'Female ejaculation' wasn't in her medical textbooks. Vanessa would have to produce proof. Her pelvic health, and her sanity, depended on it.

A Toronto writer and filmmaker in her early thirties, Vanessa had been suffering from mysterious pelvic symptoms for three years. She had begun to feel pain after sex. Yeast infections recurred over and over. She was plagued by other afflictions she couldn't explain: depression, anxiety, skin problems, weight gain. And there was a strange ache flaring up in what she called 'the spot' – it seemed near both her vagina and bladder.

Alongside the vaginal wall runs the urethra, the tube that carries urine from the bladder down and out of the body. Found below the clitoris and above the vagina, a tiny urethral opening expels urine – and in some women, roughly around when they have an orgasm, the same opening involuntarily drips, spurts or streams a different kind of fluid. It has long been a source of anguish to women terrified that they simply were wetting the bed during sex. But it tends to be odourless and either clear or milky white, and tests have shown it has a unique composition; a 2015 study led by gynecologist Samuel Salama at a hospital in Le Chesnay, France, found the fluid typically contains prostatic-specific antigen, an enzyme also produced by the male prostate gland. This is 'true' female ejaculate. The liquid women squirt is sometimes only ejaculate, but most often it's mixed with urine. Either way, some women who squirt regularly say it's satisfying in a way a regular 'dry' orgasm isn't. Theories abound on whether the reflex helps cleanse the urethra of bacteria after sex, but it has mostly been the preserve of curious bladder specialists and murky to almost everyone else, even though some assert that nearly all women have the ability to squirt.

Normally, Vanessa ejaculated every time she had sex. But now, as that ache grew, it was getting harder to come, and harder to ejaculate. She'd feel uncomfortably full of fluid. When she did come, there was more pain. It felt, she says, like 'pleasure gone wrong.' If she did squirt, the fluid smelled different. Sometimes she would cry after sex from the cramping, unsure of what was happening inside her body, why one of the things she loved now hurt. She saw doctor after doctor, but when she told them her symptoms, they didn't know what female ejaculation was.

'They kept telling me, "Nothing's wrong with you."'

In 2009, two French gynecologists named Pierre Foldès and Odile Buisson used a sonogram to create a 3-D map of the female pleasure centres. Hoping to shed light on the still-controversial 'G spot,' they scanned five volunteers with a vaginal probe, having the participants squeeze their muscles and creating sonographic images of the clitoris in motion. The images produced by their study show the full, expansive clitoral structure: its external nub, called the glans, giving way to its long legs or wings, called crura, and the bulbs, which straddle the vaginal canal like a wishbone.

Sorry – *what? Legs and bulbs?* Yes, we're still talking about the clitoris. The clit isn't just the small, sensitive pea at the top of the vulva, the rubbery nub it's normally billed as. Like an iceberg, the full clitoral structure lies mostly below the skin's surface, inside the body. In comparison to the head (glans) that's visible and touchable outside the body, the Real Clitoris is expansive, containing about as much erectile tissue as a penis. Illustrations of it resemble a swan, with arched neck, spread wings and bulbous lower body. When I saw an illustration of the clitoris's true shape for the first time I felt like a blind man finally seeing a whole elephant when all he'd ever known was the tip of its trunk.

What these bulbs and legs told the world was: *Hey, the clit is a literally bigger deal than we thought!* For women who have reached climax by massaging just their outer labia, their pubic mound or even areas inside their vagina that *aren't* the G spot, the concept that there's a lot more responsive tissue down there than previously advertised makes a lot of sense.

In one way, this 'discovery' was one giant leap for womankind. In another, however, the fact that this seemingly basic bit of anatomy was still being elucidated so recently was an unsettling reminder of how little effort society has made to understand women's body parts when the parts in question aren't crucial for making babies. As biologists and feminists alike have pointed out, the clitoris, packed with over eight thousand nerve endings, is likely the only human organ whose *sole purpose is pleasure* – unlike the penis, which is responsible for procreation and urination as well. None of this jives with Western, Christian views of proper womanhood, and that's reflected in the science. Leonardo da Vinci was lovingly sketching cross-sections of male genital anatomy back in 1493, but we haven't focused nearly as much on female anatomy. To put it another way, the mapping of the entire human genome was completed in 2003, years before we got around to doing a detailed ultrasound on the ordinary human clit.

But don't listen to me. Here's Dr. Foldès, who has performed surgery to restore sensation to over three thousand victims of female genital mutilation, quoted by New York's Museum of Sex: 'The medical literature tells us the truth about our contempt for women. For three centuries, there are thousands of references to penile surgery, nothing on the clitoris, except for some cancers or dermatology – and nothing to restore its sensitivity. The very existence of an organ of pleasure is denied, medically.' A 2005 report by urologist Helen O'Connell in the American Urological Association's *Journal of Urology* said the anatomy of the clitoris has 'been dominated by social factors ... Some recent anatomy textbooks omit a description of the clitoris. By comparison, pages are devoted to penile anatomy ... The clitoris is a structure about which few diagrams and minimal description are provided, potentially impacting its preservation during surgery.'

Ignorance isn't the whole story, however. Over millennia, we have produced a wealth of knowledge about women's sexuality; the problem is that we're very good at ignoring it. Although the full clitoral structure – whose dense connections to the urethra and uterus have led some experts to see it as part of an even larger whole, the clitourethrovaginal (CUV) complex – was mapped via ultrasound in 2009, it was described in detail over a decade before, in a 1998 paper by O'Connell and her three co-authors in *The Journal of Urology*. In fact, detailed illustrations of internal clitoral structures appeared much earlier, in German anatomist Georg Ludwig Kobelt's classic cadaver-dissection work, *The Male and Female Organs of Sexual Arousal in Man and Some Other Mammals* ... back in *1844*.

Yes, 1844 was more up-to-date on the Real Clitoris than, say, 1995. Sadly, even after so many separate 'discoveries,' the Real Clitoris isn't known to many, although a rising number of new studies mentioning it and the CUV since 2009 are sparking more (if always bewildered) reports in the media.

The essence of this centuries-long disagreement about female sexuality can be expressed in a question: is the vulva a *thing* or is it an *absence*? Is what lies between women's legs an organ, with emphasis on what protrudes: the clitoris, the labia, the eight thousand nerve endings, *flesh*? Or is it a *void*, a vessel, an opening, an orifice, a place that exists to be filled by something else? Through history, the latter view has been accompanied by violence and the erasure of women's sexual desire in favour of men's. The former has typically gone hand in hand with a view of women as sexually independent agents who experience desire, pleasure and power.

History has regularly produced remarkable insights into women's sexuality: awareness of the clitoris's role in pleasure, the female orgasm, even female ejaculation. But, whether accidentally or wilfully, we've then omitted or erased this information from the canon. We've hidden the richness and power of it for so long that even women have come to regard their own bodies as enemy territory – weird, marine, mucosal and alien. There have been repeated cycles of forgetting and rediscovering, as Naomi Wolf observes in *Vagina*, where she presents a sweeping chronology of the decline of the vulva and vagina: from millennia of being worshipped as sacred by prehistoric civilizations, to being downgraded by the classical Greeks, to being hated as profane in monotheistic societies centred on a father god.

In other words, women's sexuality began by being celebrated, then was feared as too potent, before being downplayed and denied in the scientific era. The efforts that so many women (and men) are making today to understand female sexuality are not just discovery – they're attempts at recovery and resuscitation.

A brief look at this rise and fall (and rise, and fall) inspired by Wolf will help shed light on how we got to where we are now – a time when dramatic medical advances are helping us live decades longer, and yet a medical concern like Vanessa's can go misdiagnosed for over a year because it involved a part of her that, to her doctors, didn't exist.

Early humankind revered the vulva. This was both mystical and eminently reasonable, considering human life was mysterious and the vagina was its source. (Just so we're all clear, *vulva* refers to the external female genitalia, and includes the inner and outer labia, the head of the clitoris and the introitus, or entrance, to the vagina. The *vagina* refers only to the internal canal that leads to the uterus.)

Early humans carved vulval clefts into rocks. Ancient goddesses such as Astarte and Aphrodite weren't simply prayed to for fertility, but, as Wolf points out, explicitly worshipped for their eroticism. The Sumerians, who lived five thousand years ago in what is now Iraq, worshipped the vulva of the goddess Inanna as 'a boat of heaven,' according to one hymn. The fertility of the earth was linked to sexuality: agricultural furrows were considered vulval, and lettuce was compared to the goddess's pubic hair. A Sumerian song depicts Inanna as being straight-up delighted with her vag:

> When she leaned against the apple tree, her vulva was wondrous to behold.
> Rejoicing at her wondrous vulva, the young woman Inanna applauded herself.

Female desire was thought in ancient Greece to be stronger than men's. The female orgasm and ejaculation were described by the ancient Roman physician Galen, who recommended single women masturbate for their health. Hippocrates referred to the clitoris as '*columella*,' or 'small pillar.' The word *clitoris* itself comes from *kleitoris*, the Greek word for clitoris, which is thought to stem from *kleis*, the word for key, or possibly from *kleitorizein*, which means to touch or tickle. Even Judaism, with its view of menstrual blood as unclean, acknowledges the female orgasm in the Talmud, the text that is the basis of Jewish law. It teaches that husbands should delay ejaculation 'in order that the wife may emit her seed first'; it was thought this would ensure the conception of a male child. Misogynist in aim, yet ironically lady-pleasing in effect. (A sage named Rabbi Kattina boasts at the end of the relevant passage, 'I could make all my children males!' *Oy gevalt*.)

A civilization with an even more liberal view of female sexuality was medieval, cosmopolitan Arab society. Avicenna, the great medieval Persian philosopher and medical authority, wrote about the clitoris and named it *al bathara*, meaning 'penis.' Late tenth- or early eleventh-century Baghdad – the epicentre of the Islamic Golden Age – saw the publication of a tome called *The Encyclopedia of Pleasure* by one Ali ibn Nasr al-Katib. With forty-three chapters detailing many permutations of sex – homosexual, bisexual, heterosexual – and featuring buckets of lusty women, it would have been inconceivable over in dour Dark Age Western Europe at the time, and would be risqué even today. One tale of the extremes of unrestrained female desire went thus:

> Hubba al Madaniyyah, for instance, said that one day she went out of the bath accompanied by a boy who had a puppy. It so happened that the puppy, seeing her vulva and vaginal lips, went between her legs and began to lick her organ. She lowered her body to give the animal a better chance of performing its job. However, when she had reached an orgasm, she fell down heavily upon it and could not raise herself until the helpless animal had died from heavy pressure.[3]

Even that is tame, however, when compared to the intense worship of the female sex that formed part of early tantric practice in South Asia. While 'tantric sex' means something completely different in its current, trendy incarnation in the West, its early rituals, chronicled 1,300 years ago, involved the offering of male sexual emissions (semen) to all-powerful, sometimes frightening goddesses or *yoginis*, and the consumption of female sexual excretions (known as *yonitattva* or *dravyam*) – even menstrual blood – by male adepts. The *yonitattva* or 'vulval essence' was supplied by female adepts who embodied the goddesses in rituals.

The practice helped define tantra, according to research by David Gordon White, professor of comparative religion at the University of California, Santa Barbara. In later tantric traditions, devotees performed ritual sex with the goal of reaching higher, expanded states of consciousness through orgasm – which is roughly the form in which the (rather scandalized) British colonists first heard about it, and how it eventually reached California and the tanned New Age set. But in early, 'hardcore' tantra, vaginal wetness was the royal road to God, and oral sex was a great way to produce it. This late-medieval Tamil poem, the *Kamapanacastiram*,[4] is a step-by-step cunnilingus how-to:

Like a worshipper who circumambulates the shrine
pass your tongue over her yoni
round around from left to right,
moving in ever narrowing circles
till you reach the very centre. [...]
Taking the protruding, throbbing jewel of her yoni
gently, gently between your teeth and tongue,
suck it like a suckling feeding at the breast;
it will rise and glisten, stand up from its sheath.
It will swell like a large ruby.

At a certain point, however, the party was over for the vulva. For different reasons in many different world cultures, the tides of power turned against women in general, and women's sexuality in particular.

For example, things went south for women pretty quickly in the early Christian Church. Many of Jesus's first followers despised the body, especially the female reproductive system, comparing the womb and vulva to a 'sewer' (*cloaca* in Latin). They hated it so much that authors such as Tertullian wrote entirely serious treatises in the second-century CE on whether the Son of God could really have emerged from Mary's physical body, along with the 'impure' afterbirth, and been subjected to the indignity of being breastfed by a human woman. They ended up admitting he had when they couldn't come up with an alternative. Although not all early Christians felt this way, disgust with women and sex proved tenacious.

By the thirteenth century, Thomas Aquinas, a saint and key philosopher of Christianity, summed things up neatly: 'Woman is defective and misbegotten.'

The Scientific Revolution in Europe and the revelatory discoveries of human anatomy challenged continued ignorance of the female body. Some, like Italian anatomist and surgeon Realdo Colombo, were plainly awed by its inner workings.

Colombo claimed he discovered the clitoris in 1559, describing it as 'pre-eminently the seat of a woman's delight' and theorizing that it was central to women's ability to conceive. '[If] it is permissible to give names to things discovered by me, it should be called the love or sweetness of Venus.' He even observed female ejaculation: 'if you rub it vigorously with a penis, or touch it even with a little finger, semen swifter than air flies this way and that on account of the pleasure, even with them [women] unwilling.' Sadly, the 'discovery' of the clitoris didn't require a consenting subject. Anatomist Gabriele Falloppio (after whom the Fallopian tubes were named) also claimed to have discovered the clit a few years before.

But some of science's brightest minds were outraged at the idea of a female organ of pleasure. Flemish-born anatomist Andreas Vesalius, the genius renowned as the father of the entire field of anatomy, wrote to Falloppio: 'You can hardly ascribe this new and useless part, as if it were an organ, to healthy women,' and declared it must be a pathological structure found on hermaphrodites. It was thought by his contemporaries that larger clitorises might lead women to use them for penetrative sex with other women. This explanation, that the clitoris was a pseudo-phallic birth defect, alternated in sixteenth-century culture with the notion that its growth was *caused* by deviant women touching and rubbing their genitals. Suddenly, the folk practice of discouraging girls from touching themselves had scientific justification – it could make you grow a tiny phallus! As Naomi Wolf writes, the clitoris has been getting discovered, lost and rediscovered ever since.

It has also been getting amputated ever since. Clitorises naturally vary widely in size (from five to thirty-five millimetres in length and up to ten millimetres in width, according to one 2005 study), but early modern Europe saw large ones as a sure sign of hermaphroditism or lesbianism – and as a risk to the marriageability of young women. Doctors performed clitoridectomies – female genital mutilation, in other words – on girls and women whose organs were deemed too large. In a legal case from the 1560s (recounted in *The Body in Parts: Fantasies of Corporeality in Early Modern Europe*), a French judge annulled a marriage at a husband's request after his wife refused to have her one- to two-inch clitoris removed. The practice continued well into the Victorian era, when it was performed to discourage masturbation in girls. While we may look on, horrified, at female genital mutilation as practiced today in African and Arab societies, we'd do well to remember that until fairly recently, it was part of the repertoire of Western medicine.

The mid-seventeenth century saw the rise of medical language, including a word doctors could use when referring to the external female genitalia: *pudendum*, still a part of medical terminology for the vulva today. Like most medical terms, it is borrowed from Latin: *pudenda (membra)*, '(parts) to be ashamed of,' from *pudere*, 'to be ashamed.' By the Victorian 1800s, sexual impulses in women were actively discouraged. When it came to sex, the job of a respectable wife was passive acquiescence; anything beyond that could be labelled nymphomania.

Here, colonial racism provided sexism with a convenient prop: the sexualized bodies of African slaves – depicted in European pseudo-scientific tracts as having larger buttocks, longer labia and more ravenous sexual appetites – were used as a counterpoint to the ideal of retiring, pure, asexual white womanhood. This did much to define the white female ideal by caricaturing what it was not. In 1810, a South African woman named Saartjie Baartman was brought to London, England, where she was exhibited, like a zoo animal, as the 'Hottentot Venus,' advertised as a strange attraction for her 'exotic' body: her large buttocks and what was rumoured to be her elongated inner labia. It's a perfect example of how misogyny and racism have worked through history to bolster one another, and how black women ended up at the intersection of overlapping forms of prejudice – as women and as non-whites.

In this way, what began as misogynist belief morphed into normative, 'objective' scientific opinion. Naomi Wolf quotes William Acton, a leading British authority on gynecology, who wrote in 1862, 'the majority of women (happily for them) are not much troubled with sexual feeling of any kind.'

When she's turned on, Vanessa can't hold a thought. The idea of fantasizing when aroused doesn't make sense to her, because the sensations are so strong she can't form a picture in her mind.

'I feel like I turn into a series of lines and squiggles,' she says. 'It's like – what's the word used when birds make those moving shapes as they fly together? – a *murmuration*. I see a murmuration of starlings. That's the best way I can describe it. The fabric of reality falls away.'

If pleasure comes easily to Vanessa, so does talking about it. She laughs often when discussing subjects most would find squirmy, leaning forward to find the right word to pin down an idea. As a child, she had read somewhere that there were such things as orgasms, so she wanted to have one. And she did – her first, at age eleven. She has come just from a lover's touch on her breasts, kisses on her neck, from thinking and breathing just right. 'I have seven different kinds of orgasms,' she says matter-of-factly. 'Some are quiet, but with some I speak in tongues.' It used to be common for her to climax fifteen times in a single session, she says. And since the age of twenty-one, she has squirted every time she's had sex – copious amounts of warm liquid.

'I orgasm the way I feel emotion,' she says. 'It's big and messy and embarrassing.'

Anyone who would assume that her gifts have made Vanessa's sex life great, however, would be mistaken. 'It never made me feel empowered and comfortable,' she says. 'It made me feel weird.' The problem wasn't how she felt, but how others reacted. 'One guy called me a freak of nature,' she says. The men she's dated have often fixated on her sexuality; it has, sometimes, obscured everything else about her. Seeing a woman come ten times tends to boost a guy's ego, even if it has little to do with his abilities, and guys always want more. Sometimes, men would push her limits to see how far she could go, like she was a tricked-out sports car. 'That sounds sexy in principle, but it's not. One guy kept pushing me to keep having sex for eight hours even though I wanted to sleep, though I told him I had a meeting in the morning,' she says. 'I don't feel I have control over my sexuality.'

Now, her condition was changing everything. Feeling pain after sex, she stopped having it entirely. Still, the pain got worse. She visited the emergency room, saw her family doctor and countless specialists, who all had different ideas: chlamydia, a friable cervix, a recurrent urinary tract infection. A herpes test came back negative. A doctor who diagnosed her with polycystic ovarian syndrome prescribed her hormonal birth control, which didn't help with the pain or the blood in her urine. From October 2012 to March 2014, Vanessa underwent six transvaginal ultrasounds and was prescribed seven courses of antibiotics, even though lab tests for the bacteria that causes urinary tract infections often came back negative. The medicine would relieve her symptoms at first, but then the pain would return, followed by the blood.

In early 2013, she met C. He was her match – polyamorous, intelligent, sensitive; they began dating immediately. Vanessa remembers the first time they had sex as the best of her life. After that, though, the pain returned worse than ever. She went to a walk-in clinic and got another instant antibiotic prescription, followed by another negative test for bacteria. She started telling doctors that she *knew* it wasn't her bladder. *It's the part of me that makes ejaculate*, she'd say. She'd use a term she'd heard in online sex discussion forums, *G-spot glands*, or she'd point to the spot where it hurt, a few fingers above her pelvic bone and slightly to the right. *Right there.* She'd say ejaculating had gotten harder, that orgasms had become difficult, even painful.

But there was a communication problem. The part of her that hurt didn't seem to have a name. 'When you look at diagrams of the vagina,' she says, 'there's nothing there.'

After a six-month wait, Vanessa was admitted to a well-regarded male gynecologist with an office in midtown. In the waiting room, women read magazines on comfy chairs in front of a flatscreen that showed endless *Friends* reruns. In the exam room, a rack of pamphlets advertised labiaplasty – controversial cosmetic labia-reduction surgery. Vanessa explained her symptoms to the gynecologist, an overly friendly man in his forties who made awkward small talk about her love life. She had stopped having sex months ago because of the pain, so her symptoms had died down, but she still wanted answers. When she asked about whether G-spot glands existed, he gave her a blank stare.

'He thought it was all in my head,' she says. 'That I just needed to be told I was fine, that I was attractive. He told me my pussy was "very pretty."'

That's when Vanessa did what all frustrated patients do in the age of the internet: she consulted Dr. Google. A clue soon popped up in the form of a widely cited medical paper, 'Female Urethral Syndrome: A Female Prostatitis?' Despite its question mark, it seemed to have answers none of her doctors did. Authored by MDs Ruben Gittes and Robert Nakamura, the study focused on microscopic glands in the female urethra that sit next to the vaginal wall, known as Skene's glands or paraurethral glands. The paper argued that they are homologous to the male prostate – meaning they develop from the same embryonic tissue – and are similarly subject to infections, even cancer. The paper didn't mention the glands are linked to the G spot – the sensitive spot named after German gynecologist Ernst Gräfenberg, who described it in 1950. It also didn't mention that, for some people, the area is erogenous (like the male prostate) and produces ejaculate (like the male prostate), but Vanessa connected the dots. The paper cited a gynecologic review that estimated 5 million women visit the doctor every year with symptoms in this poorly understood area, including pain during sex, and have gotten 'an astounding variety of treatments,' wrote the authors, from various tranquilizers to 'aggressive surgical excision of the peri-urethral tissue, internal urethral cutting procedures and forceful overdilations of the urethra.' A distinct anatomic feature called the female prostate should be recognized, the study concluded, so it can be properly diagnosed and treated. The study's date: 1996.[5]

Vanessa stared at the black-and-white diagrams. Where other medical diagrams had shown blank space, these showed something akin to a sinus cavity, something that could expand with fluid. 'It was the first time I saw my anatomy reflected,' she says. Excited, she brought the study to her family doctor, along with a plastic baggie containing two vials with orange lids: one filled with urine, the other with ejaculate. She declared that her ejaculate glands – Skene's glands, paraurethral glands, female prostate, G spot, *whatever* – were infected. Her doctor looked at the paper. She admitted she had never heard of the glands, says Vanessa, but she had no other ideas. (Her doctor declined to be interviewed.)

'Can you really do this ejaculating thing?' the doctor asked. 'Can you record it and show me?'

And that's how Vanessa found herself rubbing one off on her family doctor's exam table. For science.

She was finished in two minutes.

'You're done already?' said her doctor when Vanessa called her in. The operation had been dexterous – the patient had masturbated to orgasm, ejaculated and recorded a video of the whole episode, which her doctor watched with widening eyes. They turned to her two plastic vials. Vanessa's urine sample was clear. The other liquid she had brought, however, was cloudy. The key would be to test it – for bacteria, yeast, anything that would explain the genital pain and discomfort she felt.

There was one problem: a test for the liquid that came out of Vanessa's body didn't exist. Her emission wasn't one of the designated bodily fluids that come through medical labs every day – pee, blood, saliva, semen. Her doctor would have to make up something to write on the lab form.

It has been said that the Victorian era viewed the female of the species as 'the product and prisoner of her reproductive system.'[6] The fact of being born with ovaries and a uterus was the source of a woman's essential qualities – her nurturing disposition, deficient reason, heightened emotionality.

The twentieth century saw this picture get repeatedly contested and challenged, though not always to women's benefit. The father of psychoanalysis, Sigmund Freud, was a paradox. He acknowledged the existence of clitoral pleasure – unfortunately, only to classify it as an immature, larval stage of something better: the vaginal orgasm. We now know that a distinct 'vaginal orgasm' is a myth; the majority of women (around 70 percent) do not climax from intercourse alone, and those who do are getting off either because the penis is rubbing the clitoris indirectly or it's stimulating deep erectile tissue in the vaginal wall, possibly the larger clitoral structure itself (i.e., those legs and bulbs). In other words, it's all one thing (remember the clitourethrovaginal complex?), and clitoral stimulation just happens to be a far more direct and reliable way to reach it.

But Freud believed vaginal orgasms were normal, while clitoral ones were not. Women who couldn't come from penis-in-vagina sex hadn't psychologically matured past childhood, a pre-feminine stage when little girls rub their 'penis-equivalent' – their clitorises. When they first see a real penis on a brother or cousin, however, the realization that their pseudo-penis is inadequate and resentment of their own 'castration' kicks off their transition to vaginal pleasure and normal womanhood.

'Her self-love is mortified by the comparison with the boy's far superior equipment and in consequence she renounces her masturbatory satisfaction from her clitoris,' said Freud in his 1933 lecture 'Femininity.'

It's hard to imagine now, but this convoluted theory sounded reasonable to contemporaries, and it was hugely influential. It dovetailed nicely with hundreds of years of male anxiety about the clitoris as an unfeminine, hermaphroditic or phallic organ – a female organ that protrudes rather than recedes. We could call this Clit Anxiety, and it may lurk beneath the countless instances of erasure and denial of female sexuality. Freud even mused on whether clitoridectomy could be a way of encouraging women to 'progress.' His theory of vaginal supremacy reassured European men that they didn't have to fuss about pleasuring their wives; if women weren't climaxing from intercourse, it was their own problem. In practice, this probably quashed whatever enjoyment turn-of-the-century women were having by demanding they refocus on the part of sex that was far more important: the part that involves a penis.

One of the sad legacies of all this is the case of Marie Bonaparte. A princess descended from Napoleon and a psychoanalyst who was a patient of Freud's in the 1920s, she is remembered most for something other than her royalty: she is the only person known to have surgically relocated her clitoris – *twice*. Bonaparte took the superiority of the vaginal orgasm extremely seriously and chose to solve her inability to experience *volupté* (orgasm) during intercourse by going under the knife. The problem, she decided, was that her clitoris was too far away from her vagina. Women like her, she wrote, 'remain, despite all the caresses, even with all the tender gestures that should fulfill their heart, eternally unsatisfied by their bodies.' So, rather than redirecting those caresses to a place where she could actually feel them, she had a surgeon cut the ligaments of the head of her clitoris and reattach it closer to the penis's favourite place, her vagina.

When that didn't cure her 'frigidity,' Bonaparte did the only logical thing: she had it moved *again*. That didn't work either, alas. She remains a cautionary tale of what happens when you make the gender that doesn't have a clitoris or vagina the authority on both.

The inter-war period, with the Jazz Age's loose attitudes toward sex and Margaret Sanger's fight for the right to birth control, was a comparative breath of fresh air. After centuries of clitorophobia, attitudes were shifting. As science writer Mary Roach noted in her 2008 book *Bonk: The Curious Coupling of Science and Sex*, newlyweds at the time had a surprising pick of a number of swingin' sex manuals that quietly recommended 'woman above' positions, even 'genital kissing.' She quotes the 1935 edition of *Sex Practice in Marriage*: 'Should a man be unable to restrain himself and have an orgasm before his wife, he *must* keep up the clitoris stimulation until his wife has reached the climax.'

Amy Schumer couldn't have said it better.

In 1953, Alfred Kinsey, the first major American sexologist, was set to provide scientific backup for such advice with *Sexual Behavior in the Human Female*, his widely anticipated follow-up to *Sexual Behavior in the Human Male*. A biology professor who researched gall wasps, Kinsey hadn't planned to study human sexuality until he was asked to coordinate the biology component of a course on marriage at Indiana University in 1938. The rudimentary questions students asked revealed a troubling 'gap in our knowledge,' he wrote. Kinsey was unquestionably a strange bird – he was known to film his colleagues having sex in the attic of his house as part of his research, for example – but in general, his methods were groundbreakingly empirical. His team of trained interviewers did in-depth, face-to-face interviews with thousands of subjects. His 1948 study of men had been highly controversial, revealing that homosexuality was far more common in the U.S. than believed, so you can bet his plans to reveal the hidden sex lives of American women were being anticipated with bated breath – so much so that August 20, 1953, the day the press was allowed to publish reviews of the book, was known as 'K-Day.'

Kinsey had done his best to manage the press onslaught by inviting sixty select reporters from around the world to four-day information sessions months before, and demanding stories be sent to his team for fact-checking. In the pages of national magazines such as *Collier's*, *Time* and *Life*, Americans breathlessly read statistics that exploded accepted antiquated notions about female sexuality, such as the belief that women were generally uninterested in sex, that lesbians were a myth – and that the vaginal orgasm was the norm. In fact, it turned out to be the exception. Of 5,940 female subjects, only one-third reported consistently climaxing from intercourse – and even then, their partner's penis or body had often been rubbing their clitoris at the same time. Of the 62 percent who masturbated, 84 percent stimulated their clitorises and labia as opposed to 20 percent using vaginal insertion. Hilariously, once interviewers explained the effectiveness of clitoral stimulation to that 20 percent, they tended to drop their vaginal efforts altogether. In addition, 50 percent of women had had premarital sex, 26 percent had had extramarital sex by their forties, 64 percent used fantasy while masturbating, 54 percent of married couples practiced cunnilingus and 2 to 6 percent of women aged twenty to thirty-five were almost exclusively homosexual. It was a slightly different picture of wholesome American domesticity than June Cleaver would have you believe.

If the world were a straightforward place, Alfred Kinsey's report would have immediately transformed the West's view of female sexuality. But this was America in the 1950s. So, instead, there was an immediate, tidal backlash. Many authorities rejected his statistics, saying they couldn't possibly be accurate because no 'good' woman would behave this way – or, if she had, she would at least have had the decency to lie about it. Kinsey interviewed volunteers, after all, and the type of women likely to agree to answer questions about their sex lives had to be those drawn to sexual 'excesses.' As for the vaginal orgasm, its defenders retrenched, arguing that it remained the proper sexual response of 'normal' women. In 1950s marriage manuals, it was as if the clit didn't exist. The research team of Masters and Johnson, who did much to reveal the inner workings of sexual response in the 1960s (literally: they built a dildo with a camera on it to film sexual response from the inside of the vagina), concluded that vaginal orgasms were just clitoral ones in disguise – but even they prioritized peen-in-vag penetration, arguing intercourse alone should give women all the clitoral stimulation they need. Like a persistent rash, pop-Freudianism wouldn't leave women alone.

In some ways, the era's sexual liberation just raised expectations of women. Whereas before they were supposed to be passive, now they had to respond orgasmically to stimulation that did nothing for them – or worry they were frigid. It opened women up to something they still experience now, what Carlyle Jansen calls 'the pressure that comes with possibility.' One can only assume that 'faking it' was rife in the backs of psychedelic Volkswagen vans and shag-carpeted dens across San Francisco.

It's no wonder this era saw not one, but *two* hit movies that fantasized about producing orgasms on demand. In the 1968 Roger Vadim movie *Barbarella*, with Jane Fonda, a futuristic society has replaced the messiness of sexual intercourse with orgasm pills. All a couple has to do for the big 'O' is swallow the pill, hold hands, sit next to one another and close their eyes. In Woody Allen's 1973 comedy *Sleeper*, about a future where everyone has become impotent or frigid, all people have to do is enter a chamber called the orgasmatron and – presto – problem solved.

The seventies got a wicked wake-up call in the form of Shere Hite. Raised in the Bible belt but steeped in the growing feminist movement, Hite wasn't like the sexologists who'd come before her. First, she was female. Second, while studying for her PhD at Columbia, the glamorous-looking blonde had posed nude in *Playboy*. But when a typewriter ad she'd also posed for turned out to carry the tagline 'The typewriter is so smart she doesn't have to be,' Hite joined a public protest against the advertisement's sexism. Frustrated by the way men defined women's sexuality, she designed her own sex survey, mailing out over three thousand anonymous question-naires to women about their sexual responses. In 1976, she released *The Hite Report on Female Sexuality*, which showed that 70 percent of women do not orgasm from intercourse – roughly the same as Kinsey's data. The report argued that orgasms were easy for women given the right stimulation, and that women didn't need a penis – or another person at all – to climax. The report hit like a bombshell, selling over 50 million copies. Not amused by the outspokenness of their former model, *Playboy* dubbed the book 'The Hate Report.' Hite became despised and caricatured in the press as a man-hating witch. She wrote another book addressing male sexuality and the undue pressure men feel to perform, but the attacks only continued. Not surprisingly, Hite removed herself from the

American media cycle, relocating to Europe and ultimately renouncing her U.S. citizenship.

By that time, though, something else had been shifting the discourse around women's sexuality, and it wasn't the latest official study or learned opinion – it was women themselves. Lesbian and bisexual activist groups across North America and Europe were engaging in their own vibrant debates about sexuality, pleasure and sexual assault, unimpeded by hand-wringing about demoting the penis. Gay women had been getting along just fine without penetrative sex, and their growing visibility had multifarious effects on the burgeoning female sexual cultural underground. It took the form of 'preorgasmic' meetings – support groups for women who had never reached orgasm, where they were invited to look at their vulvas in the mirror for the first time.

The Birth Control Handbook, an illegal, underground sex-ed guide printed by Canadian undergraduate students Allan Feingold and Donna Cherniak at Montreal's McGill University in 1968, flooded U.S. campuses, while Susan Lydon's explosive 1970 clitoral 'The Politics of Orgasm' argued that women's subjective experience was erased by our understanding of sexuality:

> And men defined feminine sexuality in a way as favourable to themselves as possible. If woman's pleasure was obtained through the vagina, then she was totally dependent on the man's erect penis to achieve orgasm; she would achieve her satisfaction only as a concomitant of man's seeking his. With the clitoral orgasm, woman's sexual pleasure was independent of the male's, and she could seek her satisfaction as aggressively as the man sought his, a prospect which didn't appeal to too many men.

These were soon followed by *Our Bodies, Ourselves* and *Becoming Orgasmic*, books on everything from fantasizing to birth control, written by women, for women. Meanwhile, mastur-bation advocate and sex educator Betty Dodson was holding meetings where women masturbated together in a sort of naked sisterhood, straight and gay alike. And a couple of books took the unheard-of step of asking women to describe sex and pleasure in their own words: Susan (A.S.A.) Harrison's surprising and utterly funny *Orgasms*, published in Toronto by Coach House in 1974, and Justine Hill's *Women Talking* in 1977.

Vanessa was on her third plastic vial. The third trip to her doctor's office. The third time jizzing (as she calls it) in the cup. It was the lab's fault, again. They kept messing up the test, mistaking the liquid inside for pee, assuming the forms had been filled out wrong.

Vanessa was calling all the urologists in Toronto, asking about female prostatitis. Ilia Kaploun of the Toronto Prostatitis Care Centre, one of the foremost prostate specialists in the city, was the first to call her back. He laughed at her story, however, and told her flatly that women don't have prostates. He wouldn't see her. By coincidence, her family doctor then called him to consult on Vanessa's case, and he agreed to talk to them on a strictly hypothetical basis. 'If you had a case of male prostatitis,' Vanessa asked, 'how would you treat it?' He answered – hypothetically. If you were a man and you had a prostate, he said, he'd do a course of antibiotics. She'd already done plenty of those. Well, if that didn't help, he'd test for prostatitis from candida, he said. *Candida albicans*, a fungus that hangs out in almost everyone's mouths and gastrointestinal tracts, can grow opportunistically on the tongue or in the vagina if other gut flora is thrown out of balance – in immunocom-promised people, for example. It can affect the male prostate. He'd test her for that, he said. (Dr. Kaploun declined to comment on her case. 'Anatomically women have only parau-rethral glands, but no prostates,' he wrote in an email to me.)

Vanessa was immediately back at her doctor's with a vial of ejaculate to test for *C. albicans*. This time, the lab accepted the sample. They tested it the only way they could – as a urethral swab. The test revealed a bloom of yeast spores. They were in her urine as well, but 'abundant' in the ejaculate. Vanessa was suffering from high-level candidiasis, a massive overgrowth concentrated in her paraurethral glands that had caused female urethral syndrome.

'My doctor said to me, "Huh! Now I've seen everything. You were right this whole time,"' she says. The victory was bittersweet. The spores weren't just in her paraurethral glands – they were in her blood. Two years of repeated antibiotics treatments for misdiagnosed urinary tract infections had killed off too much of the beneficial bacteria in her body. The yeast had taken advantage, growing explosively and travelling from her bladder to her digestive tract to her bloodstream.

It was April 2014. Vanessa finally had her diagnosis, but the worst lay ahead. She went on thirty days of anti-fungal drugs and began a candida cleanse, a naturopathic regimen that demanded strict adherence to a finicky diet: no sugar, bread, grains, fruit, potatoes, dairy, alcohol or countless other foods thought to feed the growth of *C. albicans*. She ate salads without vinegar or lemon, plain chicken breast without season-ing, swore off restaurants. For two and a half months. The diet wasn't the hardest part, though. As the candida colonies die off, they release large swaths of toxins, causing symptoms to get worse before they get better. Vanessa's brain was fogged. 'I couldn't remember my last thought,' she says. Sex was getting worse, not better. Gradually, her orgasms faded. One day, for the first time in her life, she couldn't come at all.

'I felt like a car trying to start,' she says – a tricked-out race car with no engine. Her emotional reaction surprised her. She felt part of her femininity had disappeared with her orgasm, like she'd shaved off a glossy head of hair. 'You ask yourself, what the fuck am I worth?' she says. 'Who's going to love me?'

In early May, about a month into the cleanse, Vanessa peed an organism out of her body. 'This thing *slithered* out of my urethra. A tablespoon of white stuff in the toilet.' Naturally, Vanessa snapped a picture and fired it off to her doctor. By the time she finished the cleanse, she felt better – at least the thing was out – though a strange tightness inside remained.

That's when she remembered the bad date.

It had been January 2011, before the pain had started, and Vanessa was at a bar. She met a younger guy named Alexei. They danced, and she gave him her number and went home. He texted later that night, begging to come over. 'He texted me gentle, delicious, sophisticated sex moves he wanted to do,' she says. Alexei was persistent, and she was horny. She agreed. Once he arrived, however, she quickly realized there would be no sophisticated moves. He was a toxic brew of aggressive, drunk and clearly inexperienced. He pushed her face down onto her bed and shoved his fingers, then his penis, roughly into her vagina. She began to bleed profusely, and both he and she became smeared in blood. When he left, she – stunned and upset but not in pain – put on a pad and went to sleep.

The next morning, on the advice of her roommate, she went to the hospital. The first abrupt question from the doctor: 'Were you raped?' She was taken aback. *Me, a rape victim?* she thought. *How could that be possible?* She said, 'No.' The doctor performed a quick, painful exam and gave her antibiotics, saying it was 'probably chlamydia.' Her results came back negative, however. But by then she had stopped bleeding. She put the memory of the 'bad date' out of her mind.

Now, though, she remembered it. Vanessa realized it *had* been a sexual assault. 'He violated my consent,' she says. He had said he'd do one thing but had done something very different. With his bare hand, he had made a wound in her vaginal wall that had gone improperly treated for three years, an injury that – together with years of antibiotics – had left her sick.

Her boyfriend found the scar tissue, and her doctor confirmed it in an exam. She described it to me: 'A teardrop-shaped ridge, stark now that the swelling in the surrounding tissue had gone down, just to the right of the centre line of my body, in the smooth tissue behind my G spot, where it had been masked by countless speculums over many examinations.' She became angry. Each of her doctors had had a record of the emergency room visit but had never, over four years, made the connection. Her own brain had shut the door on this key piece of information. Vanessa felt utterly broken.

She took a break from her relationship, sought out counselling and a good pelvic-floor physiotherapist. In August, she found herself at an ayahuasca ceremony. The hallucinogenic drug revered as medicine by South American indigenous people has won increasing numbers of devotees in the West, and she sat among a group of people hoping to be cured of depression or just exploring a different, newly trendy kind of consciousness. The ceremony opened with the participants all stating their intentions; Vanessa's was to heal the wound inside her. She drank the small, acrid cup of pulpy, coffee-brown liquor, which tasted of twigs and stale tobacco, and sat. That night, as reality dissolved around her, one of the medicine women leading the ceremony walked over in the dark and touched her belly. She sang Vanessa a traditional healing song, the *icaro*, and everyone else in the room sang with her, in an impossible harmony, pulled out of their individual trips and into hers. Vanessa cried for a long time.

Two months later, she rekindled things with her boyfriend and had, she says, 'the tiniest orgasm.'

Dr. Barry Komisaruk answered the very first email I ever sent him in exactly nine minutes. When people need help with the science of sex, he's Batman.

He is already a recurring hero in the tiny but growing handful of books about female desire and pleasure. The Distinguished Professor of Psychology spoke to me from his office at the University of Rutgers, home of one of the only labs in the world devoted to studying the brain at orgasm. They use fMRI to map brain activity in women and men over the on-average seven seconds of climax. That means he's spent years trying to get volunteers to lie as still as possible inside his scanners while at the peak of ecstasy. 'I've developed a very effective head-restraint device that reduces head movement during orgasm to about 1.5 millimetres,' he tells me proudly.

A neuroscientist by training, Komisaruk first began studying the reproductive behaviour not of humans, but of rats. He found that hormones produced by stimulating a rat's vagina blocked its perception of pain. He wanted to find out if stimulation could block pain and thus reduce suffering in human women, too. But while no one had objected to his rat studies, when he proposed the same study on humans, he hit a wall: the director of the Baptist Christian hospital where he was doing research forbade him. Doing PET scans on women stimulating themselves in his lab? Absolutely not.

'There's almost no support from federal sources for studying sexuality,' he says, then pauses to sigh. 'There's a prevailing attitude that sexuality research is a waste of money.'

Once he moved institutions, he got approval from a Rutgers research review board to study the effects of vaginal self-stimulation on pain. That's when he recruited groundbreaking sexologist Beverly Whipple. Trained as a nurse, Whipple had put the term *G spot* on the map with her 1982 book with Alice Kahn Ladas and John D. Perry, *The G Spot and Other Recent Discoveries about Human Sexuality*, which presented medical evidence for the existence of an erogenous spot of erectile tissue in the front vaginal wall, between the vagina and urethra. The book also contained anecdotal evidence of female ejaculation and linked it to glands in the G-spot area. Hearing medical authorities defend the existence of female ejaculation was a revolution for women who had been shamed for peeing during sex – including countless women who had been subjected to unnecessary surgery for incontinence. It made Whipple a controversial figure, and a bright light. She wanted to learn to do formal research, so Komisaruk suggested she enroll in a PhD at Rutgers under his mentorship, and she decided to make the question of whether vaginal self-stimulation blocks pain in women her dissertation. Working with other researchers, they found, amazingly, that it did. The door was open to advanced research on sex, and Whipple and Komisaruk became a sexuality-studies dream team.

They've since tackled fringe phenomena that have helped them shift and redefine 'normal' sexuality. They've turned their scanners on women who, like Vanessa and sex educator Annie Sprinkle, can have 'thinking orgasms,' also known as 'energy orgasms' – orgasms achieved with fantasy and deep breathing only, and no physical contact – showing that their brains light up in fMRI scans largely the same way as women having run-of-the-mill orgasms. But it was a particularly puzzling case of a woman with a spinal cord injury that led them to reveal a strikingly more detailed picture of the female pleasure system. The woman had no sensation at all in her legs, lower body or clitoris. It should theoretically have been impossible for her genitals and her brain to communicate. Yet she said she could feel vaginal and cervical stimulation – even climax. Whipple and Komisaruk ultimately found that sexual sensations were taking an undiscovered route: the curving vagus nerves (vagus means 'wandering' in Latin), which bypass the spinal cord, allowing the genitals to communicate directly with the brain.

It means that even some women with spinal cord injuries can feel pleasure.

Solving this mystery inspired Komisaruk to uncover more about how women are sexually wired. Women's genital-brain connection is wonderfully complex. The nerves that carry sexual stimulation to the brain are no single-lane street – they're a garden of forking paths, with multiple winding, alternate routes. Even women engaging in standard, vanilla sex may be channelling pleasurable sensations from three or four different nerve pairs all at once. Stimulation of the clitoris travels to the brain via the pudendal nerves – the same pair that leads up from the penis in men. That makes sense when we recall that the clitoris and penis are homologous organs, developing in utero from the same embryonic phallic tissue. But women also boast three other nerve pairs that carry sexual sensations from the multiple sensitive zones in their genitalia: the hypogastric nerves branch from the cervix and uterus, the pelvic nerves lead from the vagina, cervix and rectum, and the vagus nerves lead from the uterus and cervix region.

And the latest research has found that men, although stereotyped as 'simpler' when it comes to the stimulation they like, may not be simple at all. 'We are realizing that men's genital sensory pathways may be just as complex as women's,' says Komisaruk. Sensation from the penis and scrotum zips up to the brain via the pudendal nerve pair, but the pelvic nerves also may carry sensation from deep penile tissues, urethra and rectum, and the hypogastric and vagus nerves may branch from the prostate. The idea that men's sexuality is simpler may exist only because our culture tends to focus on the penis – other kinds of stimulation are seen as fringe. But men who enjoy anal and prostate stimulation, and those who enjoy urethral stimulation (popular in the kink world as 'sounding'), are getting a whole other spectrum of heightened pleasure via their pelvic and hypogastric nerves.

The fact that there are so many pleasure pathways goes a long way toward explaining why different women enjoy different kinds of stimulation. Some women can climax from vaginal or cervical stimulation while it does nothing for others; some know exactly where their G spot is while others will poke and prod fruitlessly. Guess what: we're all normal. All women are wired slightly differently, with some nerves being slightly more or less sensitive.

Considering this cornucopia of erogenous tissue, some experts feel that focusing too much on the G spot – or any spot – does us no favours. It makes it seem as if it's separate from the clitoris and the panoply of erogenous spots inside the vagina, when in fact there are 'dynamic interactions between the clitoris, urethra, and anterior vaginal wall.' That's according to a study by a group of Italian doctors led by Emmanuele A. Jannini advocating doctors embrace the term 'CUV complex.'

'Although no single structure consistent with a distinct G-spot has been identified, the vagina is not a passive organ but a highly dynamic structure with an active role in sexual arousal and intercourse,' commented Jannini in his 2014 study 'Beyond the G-spot.'

This puts the whole G-spot debate to rest – those who say it exists and those who say it doesn't are officially both right. The G spot exists, but so do other very hot spots: there's the U spot, a patch of sensitive tissue above and around the urethra, and the A spot, located on the deep inner vaginal wall, near the cervix, and some talk of an O spot, and then of course there's the sensitive cervix itself – all producing orgasms that feel distinct. Individual women may also have hot spots all their own. It's up to us ladies to roll up our sleeves, poke around down there and find out how we're wired.

If there has been a dialectical argument over whether female genitalia is a *presence*, a thing that takes up space, or an *absence* that makes way for something else, current science certainly describes full, overflowing presence.

All these discoveries still have yet to filter into the mainstream or the family doctor's office, however, and that's a problem. It reinforces the idea that female sexuality is mysterious to the point of being opaque. *What do women want?* No one knows, not even women themselves! But what if women's sexuality is just one of the myriad natural phenomena that flower with knowledge and cultivation, like good cooking or a thriving garden? Is female pleasure really so much more complicated than using an iPad or doing your taxes? Or is it that we've ignored the vast knowledge about the female body that has accumulated over history – and then claimed, like Freud, not to know what women want?

Even those who write about female sexuality fall into this trap. 'You have no idea what a perplexing mess is female arousal,' writes Mary Roach in *Bonk*, a book that is on the whole extremely progressive and illuminating about women's bodies. Do we also say that the human brain is a 'perplexing mess,' or do we speak in hushed tones about its complexity, praising its 86 billion neurons, impressed and rather proud that we have no idea how the hell it works? What we're *really* saying when we say women are complicated, argues Emily Nagoski, is that we expect them to behave like men, with their simple erections. Women are confounding only when men's sexuality is the gold standard and women's sexuality is understood as a faulty version of that – 'defective and misbegotten.' Compare women's sexuality to that of *other women*, however, and our expectations shift.

When I first sit down in my living room with Vanessa on an afternoon in fall 2014, she asks for no sugar in her tea. 'I feel I'm going to be periodically candida cleansing for the rest of my life,' she says. Her sexual responses have dulled and shrunk, perhaps permanently. She has one orgasm now, maybe three, and worries the pain will come back. In some ways, it has given her empathy. 'I realize a lot of women can't have orgasms,' she says. 'I feel I judged them.' She hangs out in online forums where women talk about pelvic problems – inability to orgasm, pain they can't explain, vague diagnoses. 'They have the same symptoms as me,' she says. Their doctors give them painkillers and say, *Just don't have sex*. She says she's found more accurate information about her anatomy, her squirting, G-spot glands and her urethral sponge – G-spot erectile tissue – on FetLife, an online forum for people with sexual fetishes, than from any medical source. This troubles her. 'If it's not the parts of your female anatomy that make a baby, or your bladder, they don't know anything,' she says. 'How is it possible that we're so obsessed with sex – at least the functioning of men – and we're just figuring this out *now*?'

It was not obvious that what had colonized Vanessa was *C. albicans*. No one would have expected an examining doctor to look at her and guess at such a confounding diagnosis. What's troubling is that the incomplete medical literature made it impossible for any doctor to know where to begin. If a part of your patient's body doesn't have a clear medical existence, that's a problem. The fact that female ejaculation is still considered fringe science, despite study after study since 1982, and remains the hobbyhorse of online sex chat rooms rather than anatomy textbooks is frankly bizarre. Why does a part that is in millions of ordinary women have the same status as UFOs? That this is a 'mystery' is proof of lingering systemic sexism in medicine. Vanessa's example is sadly just one of many.

'I'm a stubborn, outspoken person,' she says. 'If I had been slightly less of those things, I'd have never solved this and lived with it my whole life. And just not had sex, ever.'

A growing number of women like Vanessa aren't waiting for official sources to tell them how their bodies work. They are investigating themselves.

In Barcelona, a radical feminist collective wonderfully named GynePunks, determined to reclaim the treatment of women's reproductive health, is building and maintaining its own gynecology lab. They've got 3-D-printed specula, centrifuges made of old hard-drive motors – enough to do routine tests and exams. One of their acts has been to rename the G-spot glands 'Anarcha's gland': it doesn't make sense to have it named after some nineteenth-century male gynecologist named Skene. They named it for Anarcha, one of three black female slaves in 1840s Alabama who were subjected to as many as thirty horrific surgeries without anaesthetic by J. Marion Sims, gynecologist and inventor of the speculum, so he could research surgeries to perform on white women. Racism and sexism is baked into the innocuous speculum itself – think of that next time you're in the stirrups. A typical trip to the gyno 'represents, at least for me, some kind of purgatory, sometimes hell,' said GynePunks member Klau Kinky in an interview with *Vice*.

Two thousand and fifteen – the year of the female orgasm, remember? – also saw the debut of an ingenious new educational website called OMGYES. It aims to harness information about women's anatomy to close the orgasm gap, the wide disparity between the number of men who orgasm during sex and the number of women who do. They believe those numbers don't reflect anything essential or unchangeable: it's just a matter of finding the clit. In the 2015 *Cosmopolitan* survey about the female orgasm, 38 percent of women said they weren't getting enough clitoral stimulation to come, and 35 percent said they weren't getting the right kind. In contrast, a 2014 study from the *Journal of Sexual Medicine*, led by Justin R. Garcia, found that gay women – who tend to communicate better with lovers about their needs – orgasm about 75 percent of the time with a consistent partner.

OMGYES is an online training program where real women demonstrate exactly how to bring them to orgasm, using specific, learnable techniques. Developers Rob Perkins and Lydia Daniller interviewed hundreds of women about what gets them off and worked with Indiana University sex researchers to poll over one thousand women between eighteen and ninety-five about how they make themselves come. Thirty women ultimately volunteered to demonstrate techniques on video.

'Users can also replicate the exact motions used to bring the women onscreen to orgasm via an interactive touchscreen, providing real-time feedback during what is essentially a crash course in female sexual pleasure,' read an article by E. J. Dickson on progressive news website *Mic*. It might just be the greatest use of a touchscreen ever.

'We're experiencing something of a hangover from our previous generation, where it's still hard for people to see women as sexual beings on their own,' said Daniller in the article. 'It's fairly new that women are seen as having their own desires ...' But the female body, says Daniller, 'isn't unknowable. It's nuanced and mysterious and fascinating, but it's not unknowable.'

While they draw inspiration from earlier generations of sex-positive feminists, women who fall into the millennial cohort or younger tend to have an attitude toward sexuality that is all their own. They are relaxed about their bodies and their needs in a no-fucks-given way. They fight for sex workers' rights, defend Planned Parenthood – and deflect constant online threats of violence and rape. And although much remains to be done, they are working to strengthen alliances between straight, white women's struggles and those of LGBTQ women and women of colour – voices often excluded by an earlier generation of feminists.

They also use social media to simply say and write and tweet the word *vagina*. And *clitoris*. And *period*. Over and over, unreservedly and in all caps, these long-taboo words exert great power by just appearing. While this sounds superficial, it's not when there are constant reminders of how dangerous they still are: Michigan middle-school teacher Allison Wint said she was fired early in 2016 for saying the word *vagina* in an art class about painter Georgia O'Keeffe. A Kotex television ad was rejected by three broadcast networks in 2010 because it dared utter the V-word (i.e., the place where the tampon goes). *Clitoris* remains a word rarely heard and often censored on TV – while *penis* is far less of a problem.

To Vanessa and anyone else who has owned a vulva, a vagina or a clitoris, the fact that anatomy could be the object of so much repression, misinformation and erasure through history is the real mystery to be solved.

A Still Point in the Turning World

What is an orgasm, anyway? It depends on whether you ask a
scientist, a poet or a mystic.

Except for the point, the still point,
There would be no dance, and there is only the dance.
I can only say, *there* we have been: but I cannot say where.
And I cannot say, how long, for that is to place it in time.
— T. S. Eliot, 'Burnt Norton,' *Four Quartets*

In 1976, researchers Ellen Belle Vance and Nathaniel N. Wagner conducted an ingenious sex experiment using nothing more than words. They asked forty-eight male and female college students to describe what their orgasms felt like. The students turned in vivid accounts strewn with such unscientific descriptors as 'peace,' 'tingling all over' and 'wonderfulness.' Here is a selection:

– It's like shooting junk on a sunny day in a big, green, open field.

– A building up of tensions – like getting ready for takeoff from a launching pad, then a sudden blossoming relief that extends all over the body.

– There is a loss of muscular control as the pleasure mounts and you almost can not go on. You almost don't want to go on.

– I often see spots in front of my eyes during orgasm. The feeling itself is so difficult to describe other than the most pleasurable of all sensory impressions. I suppose the words 'fluttering sensation' describe the physical feeling I get. All nerve endings sort of burst and quiver.

– An orgasm feels extremely pleasurable, yet it can be so violent that the feeling of uncontrol is frightening.

– Sight becomes patterns of color, but [it's] often very difficult to explain because words were made to fit in the real world.

After carefully stripping out any obvious words that revealed the respondents' gender, Vance and Wagner asked a panel of judges comprising both male and female gynecologists, psychiatrists and medical students if they could identify the writers' genders based on their descriptions of the experience of orgasm – what it felt like to them. The panel could not distinguish between male and female descriptions, no matter how colourful they were. Once the researchers removed gender-specific terms such as 'vagina' and 'penis,' then – other than the odd mention of a multiple orgasm – women's experience of conventional climax didn't sound discernibly different from men's.

The take-home lesson of the study was unique in the history of sex research. It revealed that our orgasms are a great unifier. In our subjective experience of conventional, single, seven-second orgasms, gender distinctions dissolve like sandcastles in a crashing wave. Passion erases difference – it's one of the wonderful things passion does. Paradoxically, however, orgasm is also a huge moment of indescribable individuality. There is a far wider range of differences among separate women's experiences of climax – even among two instances of climax enjoyed by one woman in a single day – than there are meaningful differences between women's and men's experiences. Indeed, while there are commonalities across people's descriptions of orgasm – mounting tension, intense pleasure, immense release – no single sensation is shared by every orgasm. As incredible as it sounds, not all orgasms are even pleasant. Once you sweep aside all the purple prose about earth-shaking waves of joy or showers of stars and rainbows that populates Harlequin novels, there are plenty of weird, downright uncomfortable orgasms. If every individual is a special snowflake, your orgasm is one of the most special, snowflakey things about you.

Every attempt at defining orgasm involves an asterisk. Even experts' definitions of orgasm (and there are over twenty competing ones, according to *Bonk*) have strained the dry and careful language of science. 'A variable, transient, peak sensation of intense pleasure, creating an altered state of consciousness,' begins a 2004 definition in a paper by psychology professor Cindy Meston and others in the peer-reviewed *Annual Review of Sex Research*. 'The zenith of sexuoerotic experience that men and women characterize subjectively as voluptuous rapture or ecstasy,' begins another by sexologist John Money.

Author Emily Nagoski wanted to find a broad, inclusive and user-friendly definition of orgasm with as few asterisks as possible, so she defined it as simply as it has ever been: 'the sudden, involuntary release of sexual tension.' Yet even this short, sweet take could prompt someone, somewhere, to raise her hand and object. People are that irritatingly unique. One woman interviewed by A.S.A. Harrison in *Orgasms* over forty years ago said it doesn't feel like a release; another said, 'It feels funny. I don't even know if I like them. I just find them really weird.' In a 2014 column by Anna Davies in *Elle* magazine, a woman announced with a note of proud defiance of the status quo that she has faked her orgasms willy-nilly all through her life, and was much happier that way, thank you very much, because it relieved her of the pressure to perform. 'My sex life may not have been as pleasure-packed and feminist-approved as it could have been, but at least it was authentic,' she concluded, with a particularly creative use of the word *authentic*.

What is most striking about the Vance and Wagner experiment is not that they couldn't distinguish the participants' genders. It is the near-lyrical descriptions themselves. What are these strange, life-affirming peak experiences we're all having yet don't typically bother discussing unless a nosy researcher prods it out of us? What are these magical, transcendent moments that are as common as dirt? A thousand times as much ink is spilled in the service of capturing the nuanced flavours, scents and textures of a pork belly appetizer or a $14 bourbon cocktail as that used to convey the intense moments of happiness regularly enjoyed at home. Yet for all their ordinariness, what exactly *are* orgasms?

The answer depends on whether you ask a scientist, a poet or a mystic.

The English word *orgasm* originates from the ancient Greek word *orgasmos* – 'to swell as with moisture, be excited or eager.' The ancient Greeks weren't far off in describing the physical changes that occur during arousal. As detailed earlier, both women and men have genital erectile tissue that swells and reddens during sexual play, and women have just as much of this tissue as men do, but rather than having it concentrated in one organ, theirs is distributed through the clitoris and the inner labia. All this tissue swells with moisture and excitation, getting redder, plumper, springier – often expanding to twice its normal size, hence the term that sex educators have begun to give the whole shebang: *herections*.

But swelling with excitement doesn't describe *climax*, exactly – it describes the phase before orgasm. Physiologically, what is orgasm itself? The outward indicators of the female orgasm have been lovingly debated by intrepid explorers going back to the careful Taoist sex manuals of the Han dynasty, roughly two thousand years ago. The longer time it takes women to orgasm (usually fifteen to forty minutes) wasn't a problem in Taoist thought – it was part of the balance of yin and yang. In the Taoist worldview, men had more yang and were like fire: quick to heat up and quick to cool down. Women had more yin and were like water: slow to bring to a boil and slow to cool down. The two energies balanced one another.

'At least forty-five minutes of foreplay before penetration,' says New York City integrative health educator Anita Boeninger, who has studied Eastern eroticism. 'Taoist practitioners knew a woman needs to be stimulated to the boiling point where she needs to be penetrated. *Begs* to be penetrated.'

Elaborate courtly dialogues between the 'Yellow Emperor' and the 'Plain Girl' or 'Mysterious Girl' detailed the 'Five Signs, Five Desires, and Ten Indications' of female arousal for perplexed men, according to Daniel P. Reid, author of a book on Taoism and health: 'flared nostrils and parted lips' meant a woman wished to move from foreplay to having her vulva touched; a 'parched throat' meant her lover should thrust more vigorously, and her orgasm had officially taken place when 'slippery fluids flow from the Jade Gate and her vital-essence is released.' Truly it was a golden age of sexual detective work.

Perhaps male lovers have always wanted visible assurances of their prowess. If all orgasms are mysterious, female orgasms are the most mysterious. Male orgasms typically come with an indicator that's hard to miss – semen isn't nicknamed 'cum' for nothing. In contrast, the female orgasm doesn't arrive with a name tag proudly announcing its presence and staining your rug. It is a completely subjective event, a fireworks display for one going off behind closed eyelids. The question of 'did she' or 'didn't she' begins to nag, and the hunt for evidence starts. It's no wonder that demand for female ejaculation or 'squirting' in porn is rising – it's a visible reward for hard work, a liquid jet of enthusiasm that soothes the male desire to *accomplish* something by telling him, 'Good job.' (Ironically, the popularity of squirting in porn has led to countless how-to guides. What was supposed to be a sign of unfiltered pleasure is now yet another learned performance.)

But even something that seems as obvious a sign of climax as you can get – such as female ejaculation – has been known to happen before or after orgasm, or without an orgasm taking place. Other signs aren't reliable, either. Powerful vaginal contractions that can be felt with a finger or penis accompany orgasm in some women, but they're unnoticeable in others. Some women scream when they come, but others go dead silent.

Today, a small but growing vanguard of intrepid scientists are working just as hard as the authors of the ancient Taoist manuals to track the physical evidence of orgasm. But the terrain of the hunt has shifted from the female body to the female brain.

Dr. Barry Komisaruk at Rutgers, whom we met earlier, uses fMRI to peer into the brain at the moment of orgasm. The scanner takes continuous snapshots of volunteers' brains in ecstasy – an image every two seconds. Spread over several minutes, the snapshots reveal that the orgasmic brain is like an intensifying symphony, nearly all its instruments reaching a crescendo at the peak of pleasure. Orgasm lights up almost every brain region with activity: from the hypothalamus deep in the brain's centre, which signals the pituitary gland to release oxytocin into the bloodstream, triggering muscular contractions of the uterus (rather pleasantly, to many), to the hippocampus, the short-term memory centre, which is active even in the brains of women who can 'think' themselves to orgasm without physical stimulation – suggesting it plays a role in the cognition of orgasm. (Yes, even a moment of mindless abandon has a cognitive side.)

Sex changes the brain's electrical activity, too. In a 1976 study led by researcher H. D. Cohen, electroencephalograph readings taken of people masturbating in the lab showed that their brains go from their usual predominance of beta frequencies (associated with the normal waking state of consciousness) to having increased theta frequencies, with the moment of climax associated with a big spike in theta. Since the theta rhythm is most often observed during sleep and deep meditation, that discovery prompted self-pleasure advocate Betty

Dodson to declare in her classic pro-wanking book, *Sex for One*, that masturbation was a practical, fun form of meditation – to the horror of some Buddhists.[7]

The neurotransmitter that plays the starring role in the brain during the hedonic rush of orgasm is the same one involved in the high experienced by cocaine and amphetamine users: dopamine. It surges through the brain's receptors in response to rhythmic, repetitive stimulation of the genitals and other erogenous zones, sensitizing the brain to sexual stimuli. Research shows that dopamine doesn't simply flip an orgasm switch, however – rather, it augments the sexual signals that are there.

This hints at the difficulty of coming up with a female Viagra. There is no single chemical that 'turns us on.' Giving female rats dopamine has actually produced the opposite result, seeming to inhibit some mating behaviour. (Females of many species are delightfully complicated.) The gush of dopamine pleasure is kept in check by the inhibitory action of serotonin, the 'brake' of the hedonic reward system. This is thought to be the root of one of the saddest common side effects of antidepressants such as Prozac and Celexa, which increase levels of available serotonin in the brain: loss of libido and difficulty with orgasm.

As sexual stimulation continues, more and more of the brain's neurons get invited to the sexytime party. That's when the magic of orgasm's brain-body waltz truly unfolds. Signals are sent from the brain to the many muscles in the belly: the pelvic floor, or Kegel muscles, which control the womb's contractions. Their movements send ripples through the body. This generates *more* sensation, pouring more pleasant sensory input back into the brain. This is a cycle known as 'reafference.' It is this positive feedback loop between brain and body – 'a cyclically building cascade of sensory stimulation,' as Komisaruk and his book's co-authors, Beverly Whipple and Carlos

Beyer-Flores, put it – that, when all systems are go, piles pleasure atop pleasure and creates that feeling that all the sensations in your body are building toward explosion.

Just because it involves a muscular response, though, doesn't mean orgasm is just a reflex, like a sexual sneeze, point out the authors of *The Science of Orgasm*. The key to this feedback loop is that all this stimulation has to feel *good*. Orgasm is a *perception* – it takes place in the mind, not the muscles.

Is the female brain any different from the male brain during orgasm? The question is surprisingly fraught with disagreement. Our brains are remarkably similar at climax, but there's one difference, related to one little neurohormone: oxytocin. It's been called 'the cuddle hormone' and even 'the love drug' for the role it plays in childbirth, breastfeeding and social bonding, and it also plays a role in sex, causing uterine contractions. Vaginal and cervical stroking prompts the brain to release oxytocin, and a big, sudden spurt of it enters the female bloodstream within a minute after orgasm. A 1994 study, led by researcher Marie Carmichael, of multiorgasmic women showed that the more intense their orgasm, the more oxytocin was in their systems afterward. Men also produce oxytocin before and during orgasm – it even helps erection take place – though at climax, it's released more gradually. But although there are theories that it could influence feelings of trust in women, scientists don't know this for sure. That hasn't stopped newspapers and relationship coaches from warning women about being deceived by the rush of oxytocin, which could make them adore the bad boys they've fallen into bed with. (Men don't get those warnings, for some reason.)

The bigger difference lies in the female body, not the brain. As mentioned in Chapter Two, sexual stimulation travels through four different choose-your-own-adventure nerve pathways that run from the clitoris, vagina, cervix, uterus and the skin around the vulva. Women have 'a unique and richly developed pattern of sensation,' say *The Science of Orgasm*'s authors, and it can be stimulated using various techniques – with plain ol' peen-in-vag sex, with oral sex, with fingers, with toys. Many women describe clitoral orgasms as sharp, fast, explosive and more centred in their genitals. Vaginal orgasms, by contrast, have been described as deeper and spreading throughout the body, as are 'blended' orgasms – those from simultaneous vaginal and clitoral stimulation.

'If we're going to categorize orgasms by how they feel,' writes Nagoski in *Come As You Are*, 'we'd need a new category for every orgasm a woman has.'

Women's orgasms are so richly varied that it has prompted Komisaruk, Whipple and Beyer-Flores to argue that they can't be an evolutionary by-product of men's orgasms, the way the male nipple is the by-product of its evolution in women. This is probably the most well-accepted current theory for why the female orgasm evolved: that the male orgasm helps spur ejaculation and, thus, impregnation, and thus, continuation of the species; women's orgasms, which aren't crucial to conception, tagged along for the evolutionary ride. There's nothing wrong with that account, which evolutionary biologist Elizabeth Lloyd has dubbed the 'fantastic bonus' theory. Some have objected that it denigrates female pleasure, but in some ways it's quite the opposite. Unlike male pleasure, which evolved to make babies, ours just *feels good, man*. It serves no purpose but its own.

Other scientists, however, have offered up intriguing theories. Komisaruk and company argue there is evidence that the uterine contractions of orgasm help 'suck' sperm up and into the womb, which would support old folk wisdom that the female orgasm aids fertility. There is also the rather more simple theory that orgasms motivate women to have lots and lots of sex, and thus procreate.

The debate continues.

The authors of *The Science of Orgasm* point out an even more subtle wrinkle to all this: *men's orgasms are also mysterious*. It seems as though guys come for an obvious evolutionary purpose: to produce semen. But the authors point out that men do orgasm without ejaculation – and ejaculate without orgasm. They write that 'viable, pregnancy-producing' spaff has been produced by men with spinal cord injuries who can't feel pleasure at all.

'[T]here is no better adaptational explanation for the existence of men's orgasm than for the existence of women's,' conclude the authors. It makes sense that ejaculation would evolve to feel good, but there's no evolutionary reason for it to feel *that good*.

Despite all this pioneering research, Komisaruk, Beyer-Flores and Whipple point out that what brain science can tell us about orgasm is ultimately limited. Although there will gradually be more and more complete models of what happens in the brain during ecstasy, it still won't be able tell us which neurotransmitters or group of receptors *cause* the perception of orgasm – because there is no model of how the brain 'causes' *any* state of consciousness.

'Neurons are a bag of chemicals, and subjective experience is something else,' Komisaruk tells me, explaining that he first wanted to study the brain not to figure out women's orgasms, but to solve neuroscience's biggest Gordian Knot: what is consciousness? That mystery remains as tightly knotted as ever, however. 'There are 50,000 neuroscientists in the world now, and no one has a concept of [how a neuron produces awareness],' he says. (Komisaruk ended *The Science of Orgasm* with a theory that consciousness exists in another dimension inaccessible to physical science. Pretty philosophical for a book about spooge.)

Orgasm is a special state of consciousness. We need only to experience it to know that. It's just as different from normal waking consciousness as are dreaming, trance, intoxication or deep meditation. How to describe that in terms of brain activity, however, is still a mystery. Scanners can't yet tell us why you have the kind of orgasm where it feels like you've left planet earth, oblivious to all around you. Or the kind you feel more in your heart than in your vag – where your chest bursts almost painfully with emotion, making you feel more deeply in the world than ever before. All science can tell us is what's happening in our bodies – in our grey matter, our ducts and nerves and guts – when we climax. It can't tell us the rest of the story: what that bizarre moment means to us.

Literature, culture, religion and mysticism – as with so many of the most important realms of life – step in where science leaves off.

English-speaking folk have borrowed a term from the French, *la petite mort*, to refer to orgasm since the Victorian era. It means both the loss of consciousness that seems to take place at the peak of climax, as well as the brief period of exhausted unconsciousness that can come right afterward (if perhaps in men more than in women), as the life essence drains away. It has been thought of as a moment that prefigures death, *la grande mort*. Whether a gush of serotonin (the 'brake') is responsible for the *mort*, it's impossible to say. Rather, we should listen to French novelist Georges Bataille:

> From her stare, then, at that moment, I knew she was drifting home from the 'impossible' and in her nether depths I could discern a dizzying fixity. The milky outpouring travelling through her, the jet spitting from the root, flooding her with joy, came spurting out again in her very tears: burning tears streamed from her wide-open eyes … there was nothing that didn't contribute to that blind dying into extinction.

This concordance of ecstasy and the grotesque in his novel *Madame Edwarda* isn't most people's experience of climax (thankfully), but some do feel a 'blind dying into extinction.' For Naomi Wolf, orgasm is far more positive, with the potential to heighten 'euphoria, creativity and self-love.' She has a pet theory that good sex stimulates women's original thinking, and that creativity stimulates more good sex. Orgasms, to her, are feminist.

Putting an orgasm into words is a little like attempting to describe the moon reflecting off a lake through mist – it is a challenge to speak about a subjective perception available to no one but the person having the experience. It is a feeling of oneness that isolates us. Sexologists are in good company with novelists, poets, phenomenologists, Buddhists who describe their deepest meditative states and psychonauts who write accounts of LSD trips: they're all trying to translate exceptional sensory experiences into dull words.

An orgasm is like a little death because it is a lost moment in time, a second in which consciousness briefly flickers, wrote (the also very, very French) Catherine Clément, philosopher and mistress of *écriture feminine*.[8] She declared that sexual orgasm was a form of 'syncope' – a word that in medicine means fainting, swooning, a skipped heartbeat or loss of consciousness, but (particularly in French) can also refer to a missing sound or syncopated beat in music or poetry. It is not a thing, but an absence. The world falls away. It's a moment where we 'lose our heads,' along with our certainty that we're autonomous subjects occupying a specific point in time and space. '[T]he mooring ropes that hold fast the subject' are cast away, she writes in *Syncope*.

But where do we go during orgasm? Where have we disappeared to? Do women fall further, slip away to a more mysterious realm? One writer who has tried to answer those questions is Mikaya Heart. Heart was not a sexologist, but she didn't let that detail stop her. A self-described shaman, a polyamorous lesbian, a dedicated nomad (she built a house herself in California years ago, then sold it when she felt that owning property tied her down) and the author of several books, including *When the Earth Moves: Women and Orgasm,* Heart wanted to answer questions that lie beyond science: Why do people report that orgasms feel spiritual? Can an orgasm change your life? What does love have to do with it, if anything?

Human sexuality right now is a little like mathematics at the time of Euclid or physics during the Renaissance: an inchoate field we've studied in such a patchy, inconsistent way that a curious generalist can still make an original contribution, scientific credentials or no. In the 1990s, a new era of feminism, heated culture wars and sexual identity politics, Heart was determined to understand her own complicated relationship with sex. She interviewed twenty-three friends and friends of friends, and circulated a questionnaire online. Many of her subjects were, like her, lesbians – and thus, she figured, probably more deeply acquainted with female sexual response than most. Nearly two decades after it was published in 1998, her book still feels new. Now in her sixties, Heart remains one of the great sex researchers that nobody has ever heard of. I had to give the feisty ethnographer of the female orgasm a call.

Heart spoke to me from the cabin she was staying in on a friend's land in Arizona, one of the closest things to a permanent residence she says she can stand. Her voice still carries a hint of the brogue of her native Scotland, and is sweetly girlish, as if she hasn't aged since her twenties. She rarely does interviews, she says, but she is jazzed at my nerdy enthusiasm. She begins to tell me about her first orgasm.

She was twenty-six or twenty-seven, living in Wales, and her life was in flux. As a young girl, she'd been sexually molested by a family friend, and for decades after, she could never understand why such an ugly act was called 'making love.' She had recently gotten entangled with a woman for the first time – but that woman was married to a man. 'Of course, he wasn't very pleased,' she says. In fact, the husband threatened to kill her, and Heart ran away from Wales to the continent. While staying with friends in Switzerland, she revealed to one of them that she'd never had an orgasm – the sensations always got too uncomfortable and she had to stop. The friend insisted she masturbate, and persevere.

'One night, when the tension in my body built to that now familiar place, I gritted my teeth and kept going,' she wrote in *When the Earth Moves*:

> My shoulders, my neck, and my belly became as tight as iron and I felt as though I was going to explode – and it wasn't going to feel good … I had a sense that something astonishing, something much more powerful than I was carrying me like a wave, and then it flung me down on the shore … my clitoral area felt like it had been burnt, I was trembling all over, and I wanted to cry. I curled up and held myself, comforting myself with the thought than I never had to do this again.

For Heart, the climax was not a happy ending – it was a searing ordeal. Soon after, however, she came out completely as a lesbian and fell in love with a woman for the first time.

That experience, along with conversations with dozens of women, led her to her contrarian theory about why female orgasms can be elusive, one I've heard nowhere else: that some women don't have orgasms because, on some level, it's not the right time:

> There are usually very good reasons why a woman will block a certain flow of energy at a particular time … It may be that women who don't come or don't come easily, are not psychologically ready to experience what the orgasm will do to them: that intense, shocking alignment of body and soul that can occur with a strong orgasm.

Orgasm as a life-changing experience? 'We're so attached to leading lives that are consistent and predictable,' she says, and a big orgasm is a flood of energy that can break an emotional dam. It can also be a healing tool, triggering realizations about changes that need to be made. Women shouldn't feel pressured to come, she says – they'll do it in their own good time. If that time never comes? No big deal.

It sounds crazy, but if true, it would help explain why some of the women I'd met while researching this book had gotten close with their Hitachi Magic Wands, only to stop at the cliff's edge, bursting into tears.

Robyn Red, a Toronto body worker who does a combination of sexual massage and healing touch, agrees. She says that for her clients, both male and female, orgasm is often a precursor to a psychological and emotional release. 'The orgasmic explosion of emotion can push things through much faster,' she says. She tells the story of a client who, right after he climaxed, reliably had major epiphanies about his life, his dead-end job and old issues with his father. In his last session with her, he said happily that he was leaving his job.

The mostly gay women Heart surveyed for her book described a variety of orgasms with glorious, unselfconscious weirdness. Some said they had to be in love to come, others said it was hottest with a stranger. She devoted pages to which colours women see when they come, to sleep orgasms and whether orgasms can induce labour (answer: sometimes!). There were 'disappearing orgasms' that die on arrival. 'Some even verge on boring but necessary ...' said one woman. 'I feel like my whole body has been hit with a baseball bat ...' 'I am exploding in a ball of blue light, an intense deep blue ...' 'I normally have probably five to seven, and the third and fourth are the strongest.' One woman couldn't handle more than one, because hers were 'like a seizure; they pick me up and throw me around.' One said she once came just from listening to music, another from watching horses race.

Based on her interviews, Heart tried to identify several new categories of female orgasm:

Flying
Wave
Falling
Surface
Deep
Disappearing
Crying
Throbbers
Veets
Blips

… before giving up and declaring the exercise pointless.

Why is it that simply asking women about their sexual experiences – not voyeuristic confessionals about getting trashed and having sex, but subjective feelings – seems radical, even political? Describing the sheer, encyclopedic variety of women's experiences does more than just satisfy curiosity. It defies the assumption that there's some 'normal' experience of sex out there, and allows others to venture beyond what they've been told it's supposed to feel like. We're *all* outliers. Seeing language that expresses the variety of human experience has the power to help us accept how we feel.

Seen this way, the complexity of the female orgasm is a gift – it demands women and those who love them be creative, curious and empathetic in the bedroom – and revealing it is powerful. A cultural shift toward welcoming this complexity might make sex less predictable and porn-mechanical – for women and men.

Today's reawakening of sex-positive feminism has spawned new curious sexual naturalists. An anonymous blog recently appeared called How To Make Me Come, which collects (you guessed it) essays by women about what makes them climax. The dizzying array of brutally honest confessions and descriptions by women of their sexuality has hit a nerve. If anything, what's new is how much more women today feel pressured to be orgasmic, a pressure that has ratcheted up over the decades. One woman described a boyfriend who always got angry at her for not coming as fast as he wanted her to: 'You made me not only feel bad, but also *ashamed* that it wasn't happening. As if your frustration would make my body be like "fiiiiiine, we'll come for you, you motherfucker."' The blog went viral in 2015, landing its anonymous editor in *New York* magazine. In a Q&A with author Dayna Evans, she said she started it after a discussion about orgasms with a friend left her 'buzzing' and thirsting to have such vulnerability in a conversation on a larger scale. Asked if she was out to demystify the female orgasm, she said something in marked contradiction to the how-to, quick-fix, life-hacking ethos of our age: 'I almost feel like this blog might mystify the female orgasm even further – it's showing that there are a million possible answers to the same question. But if there's one big takeaway from this project, it's that how to make "me" come is different from how to make "her" come.'

The cover of the April 2015 issue of *Cosmopolitan* promised, '63 Secrets to Better Orgasms: Get Over the Edge!' The words were tucked in next to the photo-enhanced cleavage of Hilary Duff, who was bending forward at an unnatural angle. Was the number sixty-three some magic, ancient tantric sum that meant 'happy vulva'? Versions of the magazine in other, perhaps more conservative, markets featured the exact same cover, but this instead: '63 Secrets to a Love that Lasts.' Sometimes a number is just so awesome, the topic doesn't really matter.

Inside, a photo showed the orgasm story's putative audience: a lineup of desperate-looking, orgasm-starved women.

Dressed as Olympic runners, complete with athletic gear and numbers on their chests, they were striving and stretching toward the finish line, teeth gritted and nostrils flared. It was perhaps more accurate than intended. The women looked pathetically sad – harried females sweating it out in beds everywhere, sprinting madly to get this sex thing over with. Even sadder, they were posed as if they were racing to beat each other. *'Hey, Samantha, guess what? New time with Brad last night: five minutes, forty-six seconds.' 'Dammit, Briony! I'm stuck at fifteen minutes! Keith and I really need to have a talk.'*

Sex for the modern woman is not so much an enjoyable release of stress and tension, or a time to simply do whatever the fuck she wants, but another sphere in which to evaluate her performance. Unfortunately, the game of who-comes-fastest is one in which most men will have the advantage. It's no surprise women often say they're too tired for sex.

Too bad, since helping us relax is one of sex's greatest benefits. We're always looking for ways to turn off the mind, with its tendency toward anxiety and obsessive thoughts, whether it's by zoning out in front of an action movie or smoking weed. Pleasure, like pain, cancels out thought. Intense sex is a great way to briefly forget your never-ending to-do list, because you can't remember the bullet points if all you can do is make guttural grunting noises. But to others, this might be the part that makes sexual surrender difficult. How do we stop thinking enough to *get* there? We might gamely try to fall into the throes of ecstasy, since we hear it's good for stress, but we think too much about whether we're doing something right, whether our partner is turned on or whether we look good. (*Cosmopolitan*'s 2015 orgasm survey found 32 percent of women say they worry so much about how they look during lovemaking that it makes climaxing harder.) Or we keep an eye on our blinking smartphone or on the mess the kids are making. We remain vigilantly rational.

Orgasm is hard because it involves surrender – briefly but completely letting go of the reins we feel we must hold tight at every moment.

One of the most common impediments to relaxing into an orgasm is pressure. We have gone from a glancing awareness of the female orgasm (back in the day, we'd be lucky to hear a *Was it good for you, too?*) to seeing it as a box we need to tick. Somewhere along the way, orgasm became to women what an erection is to men – a one-size-fits-all measure of sexual functionality, and a source of feelings of inadequacy if it doesn't appear on cue.

A big attraction of orgasmic meditation is that it demotes the climax from its central place in sex - and that takes the pressure off. It does this by redefining the word *orgasm*. For OM lovers, all women are 'orgasmic' as soon as they feel the slightest hint of pleasure. The peak at the end? That's called 'climax.' The result is that all moments of pleasure, whether tiny whispers or supernovas, are 'orgasmic.' It may sound like sexual Newspeak, but male and female practitioners say it's effective at creating a psychological shift. Now, they're no longer gunning for some goal down the road – they're reoriented to the sensations that are already there in the present moment, whatever those are. Because pleasure is a perception, not just a physical reflex, the act of paying attention to sensation can often make it more intense – leading, for many women, to easier climaxes.

The best way to reach orgasm, then? Don't worry about reaching orgasm. (Men can also experience difficulty with orgasm – it isn't just a female thing. The idea of putting less pressure on ourselves could be good for them, too.)

This may be the key to orgasms – and to sexuality in general. Forget about orgasms. Forget about goals. Just enjoy what's in front of you. Take your time. That, say some therapists, is how a more female-centred approach to sex – like that espoused by OneTaste's orgasmic meditation – could improve and expand our culture's conception of sexuality.

Shinzen Young isn't an obvious person to ask about sex. A lifelong teacher of mindfulness meditation, he travels the continent running silent retreats where busy Americans come to sit motionless from morning till night, paying close attention to their every breath and thought. There, sex is on a list of discouraged acts – sexual desire clouds the mind and distracts from meditation. Still, on a recent retreat, I asked the seventy-plus-year-old veteran of Buddhist monasteries in Japan whether orgasms could have spiritual significance.

'It is the jewel in the lotus,' he answers, without hesitation. 'It's covered over by the surrounding petals, but at its core, orgasm is an experience of empty merging with the other. It's what people *really* want. We get interested in the petals of pleasure, and that's okay. But what we really want is the jewel of emptiness and oneness at the centre.'

If none of that makes much sense, it is a little clearer in the context of Buddhist thought. One core teaching is that emptiness is a basic aspect of the universe, and some meditation practices involve training oneself to become more and more attuned to that emptiness. The student notices moments when sounds come to an end, or when thoughts disappear. She notices the end of each breath. Then, one day, the student notices that she herself is empty – that the 'self' she always thought was running the show isn't there. That's one way of describing what's known as a 'cessation,' a moment where the self disappears and the meditator has built up enough precision and clarity to notice it happen. She briefly flickers out of existence, going off-line and then instantly rebooting. It's a moment that's said to liberate the practitioner from suffering.

It's heady stuff (or bizarre, depending on your outlook). But to Young, an orgasm is just what so many meditators are looking for: a big piece of emptiness. What Catherine Clément calls a syncope. A moment where we cease to exist as functional, separate selves with identities, opinions and tax payments. It's not clear what we are then, but we're not ourselves. Or perhaps we are larger than ourselves. Indistinguishable, as Vance and Wagner found in their climax-describing experiment, from anyone else.

'That's why it's called *la petite mort*,' explains Young. 'Your space and the other person's space merge.'

It is 'a death of the self at a small scale,' said Carlyle Jansen to the women at her workshop at Good For Her, as if to explain why it seemed so scary. 'The challenge to a meditator is to maintain enough mindful clarity and equanimity during a climax – enough to notice the freedom from self,' Young says. It's easier to meditate through pain than through pleasure, because pleasure is 'stickier.' (I got the sense he'd tried.)

It may sound like heresy to some Buddhists, but Young isn't the first to link mystical feelings of merging with sexuality. 'All you have to do is go to Rome to look at Bernini's statue to see that there is no doubt, she is orgasmic (*elle jouit*),' wrote psychoanalyst Jacques Lacan, in *Encore*, of the famed Baroque statue of the ecstasy of St. Theresa. Taoist tradition teaches ways to channel orgasms into new energy that is believed to nourish the brain, warning that men who ejaculate too often will age prematurely. Tantric practices aim at similar goals, teaching how to draw sexual pleasure up the spine to the head to spur higher states of consciousness.

This may sound fanciful, but not when you think about what orgasms actually feel like – 'otherworldly,' as a friend of mine says. My first felt like I was dying, and it freaked me right out. I felt weightless, yet pinned to the bed by an unknown force. I truly didn't know what was happening. Everyone warns you that sex can lead to STDs, but no one warns you that sex may make you feel like you're suddenly disappearing. I was invaded by a spreading, exquisite numbness. Blue light was everywhere. *I'm dying*, I thought, *and this is how* EMS *is going to find me*. My shrugging acceptance of death at the time has made all the New Age tantric stuff I've heard since seem reasonable.

The female orgasm is a particularly strange beast: a bodily event that straddles nature and culture, and a biological phenomenon that requires education, inner acceptance, even skill. In my teens and twenties, I found climax tricky to reach, even under the best of conditions, so I know that if I had lived just sixty years ago, when an appreciation of the clitoris was harder to come by, I would most certainly have lived my whole life – gone through puberty, married, borne children and grown into an old Jewish woman – without having a single orgasm. I wouldn't have known what they were, and I don't think I'm alone in that. An accident of birth, history and culture mean I get to have a physical experience that seems basic to being human.

Are we any closer to understanding this near-universal yet universally inexplicable phenomenon? Is it a loss of consciousness or a glimpse of a higher one? A prelude of death or a burst of pure life force? A fantastic bonus or a laborious requirement?

It's all those things, depending on your perspective. But I like the idea that this visceral, earthy eruption somehow gives us a foretaste of something beyond the physical. We can't interview people about what dying feels like – at least, not those who die successfully. But we can ask people about all their little deaths.

4

Play

Girls just wanna have fun. They're doing just that, and it's blurring the lines between therapy, porn, health care, mysticism and prostitution. Welcome to today's wild and shameless female sexual underground.

Women are profound and mysterious – and obscene.
– author Jane Bowles, letter to her husband, Paul

In a geodesic dome, its hexagon-shaped gaps festooned with translucent red-and-yellow cloth, about two hundred dusty, sunburnt people sit cross-legged on the bare earth. The dome could be found on official maps as roughly at the intersection '2:30 and Biggie Size,' near one of the outer edges of the circular, temporary metropolis called Black Rock City, where all-day psytrance raves, anti-government surveillance education seminars and a spiritual temple larger than the average church all jockey for space with middle-aged couples' RV and ripped tents. Rows of dust-covered bicycles stand locked at the dome's entrance, each decorated with a tangled rainbow nest of lights, plastic flowers, fun fur and electroluminescent wire, which will make them glow in the night. For now, it's a scorching day. Thumping house music makes its way to us softly across the sun-baked salt flats, as giant art cars with mobile sound systems make their distant, circular parades.

I'm seated inside in the dust, surrounded by thick, curvy women with burlesque, black-and-white striped Beetlejuice stockings, skinny young men with heads shaved but for a few beaded dreads dangling from the tops of their skulls, white-bearded, shirtless old men with sunburnt, leathery necks and the odd guy in basic jeans and a tank top, looking out of place.

A woman behind me scrapes her fork in a metal container of quinoa and kale.

A young man and woman at the front of the dome introduce themselves as Keenan and Rachel (names changed upon request – she has a conservative day job) from OneTaste, the San Francisco organization dedicated to teaching the unusual, wildly popular clit-stroking art of orgasmic meditation. It claims to have attracted tens of thousands to online classes and centres in thirty cities around the world, and it's spawned stories in the *New York Times* and *Cosmopolitan*. Everyone knows why Keenan and Rachel are here: they're about to present a live demonstration of a woman in orgasm – here on this Thursday in August 2013 at Burning Man, an anarchic arts and music festival in the Nevada desert that draws 70,000 revellers and dreamers each year. In the middle of Black Rock City (the ephemeral town that 'Burners' consider themselves citizens of during the week it's fully built, complete with street grid and bylaws), Keenan and Rachel are going to try to capture the attention of a party famous for its nudity, hard drugs and wide range of sexual kinks.

Rachel sports a miniature top hat perched on her dark hair and a corset, her chest and head held high, surveying the masses. It can be safely said that she is *strutting*.

'I had this whole plan,' she begins. 'I was going to be a schoolteacher and I was going to be a *lesbian*.'

There are laughs, cheers.

'That was the plan! 'Cause I didn't really want to be intimate with men. I had unfortunate experiences with men in my late teens and early twenties. I was gonna be a lesbian. I wouldn't have to think about sex or relating to people or going after my desires.' Lesbians don't think about any of that, apparently.

She continues: 'The idea of it was great. But in actuality, I was bored. I was tired and wired. I ate too much, drank too much, dieted too much. I was miserable and couldn't figure out why. I found OneTaste. What I found was a quality of attention I couldn't find anywhere else. We go to happy hour and we talk about the weather and we talk about sports, but we never get to really *connect*! What I found at OneTaste were people who are connecting in a way I don't really see in the world. And they got there by doing this practice that I thought was *really fucking weird*. What, you guys are stroking each other's genitals all the time? No way! But I gave it a try. Once I did, I was pretty amazed with what I found, which was a well of energy and connection I haven't seen anywhere else!'

The description of this demo in the Burning Man guide promised a woman in orgasm – right here, very soon. One of the innovations of OM, however, is its redefinition of the term. As mentioned earlier, because so many women find it difficult or impossible to come, especially with the ultra-light and subtle finger stroke that is OM's trademark practice, Nicole Daedone, the guru-ish leader of OneTaste, has declared that *every* moment of pleasure a woman feels should be deemed 'orgasmic.' What we would typically call the 'climax' should be nothing special – just a point of interest on the journey. Devotees say it's a mental shift that effectively alleviates the pressure to 'get there,' and the feeling of failure when it doesn't happen. It refocuses the mind on the pleasure that's actually there as opposed to what they think *should* be there. Like meditation, it helps women and their partners (who also tend to feel pressure to bestow an orgasm) stay in the moment, rather than fixated on some elusive future goal.

'Like meditation, it looks simple on the outside.' Keenan, a slender man in his twenties, takes his turn to speak. 'Today, we're going to give you some of the nuts and bolts so you can walk out of here and be ready to attend an OM session. She has the right to say yes or no to an OM, I have the right to say yes or no to an OM, like we're asking for a cup of tea. Afterwards, there's going to be no "owesies." I'm not stroking her clit to get her to have sex with me, or to get her to buy me dinner. I'm stroking her clit because I want to. I'm getting pleasure from it. Any questions?'

There is a call for them to speak louder.

'What we're doing at OM is we're taking some of the social conditioning out of sex,' calls Rachel, loudly. 'So you know how sometimes a guy will take you out to dinner, and afterwards you'll get back to his house and think, "Oh god, now I have to do this thing."'

There is laughter in the audience.

'Or he'll go down on you, and then he'll be waiting expectantly, and you'll think, "Oh, now I have to suck his cock."'

More laughter.

'What? You guys know what I'm talking about! Come on, ladies. *How many ladies here have sucked a cock they didn't want to suck?*'

There is loud laughter.

'*Too many!*' yells someone near me.

'Raise your hand! Almost every lady's hand should go up. We've all done it! Maybe some dudes, too! We all do sexual things we feel we have to. One of the tenets of OM is *desire*. You only have an OM if you desire to have an OM. If you're stroking, you're stroking the clit for your own pleasure. So, gentlemen, you're stroking for your own pleasure, because it feels good to your finger, *not* because you want to get something from her. In the same way, the woman is sitting down for the OM because she wants to get stroked, not because she wants to appease him or do something for him. Because of that, you're not going to moan to show him he's doing it right. You're not going to flail your hips. You'll basically lie there, and if a moan comes up, awesome, and if it doesn't, awesome. It doesn't matter.'

This fun activity sure sounds like it has a lot of upfront rules. Where's the spontaneity if you have to do everything but sign a contract first? As critics say of nudist colonies, laying it all out there, as it were, ruins the mystery that helps make sex, well, *sexy*. But the young firebrands before us have a counterargument. Sex is already weighed down with centuries of illogical unspoken rules, expectations and trade-offs, mostly dumped onto females. So much so that a lot of women end up saying, *Sorry, this isn't worth the trouble*. They're sold spontaneity and ecstasy, then hear, *Oh, by the way, you must play hard to get, don't be too eager, dress sexy but not slutty, act like you're enjoying it or you'll hurt his feelings and don't be the first one to text afterward. Have fun!*

So what if someone invented new rules that women can feel good about – rules that are, at least, transparent? And what if the first rule was *Don't do sex if you don't want to*? In the space of total permission to say no, would a yes emerge?

Vibrant, female-dominated sexual subcultures are growing in response to the persistent sexual myths that still harm women's health, as seen in Vanessa's story in Chapter Two. While drug companies spend millions in the search for a pill or hormone that will zap women's brains into summoning more desire for the sex they're currently having, some women are stoking their desire by seeking out new and improved sex. Inspired by the feminist awakenings and clitoral manifestos of the 1970s, fed by the massive yoga and natural health boom and the hippified music-festival circuit, women across North America, Europe and beyond[9] are trying unconventional practices, sex-positive gatherings and holistic experimental therapies. Many of the same young women protesting against Wall Street and tweeting about rape culture and marching in SlutWalks are also engaging in radical, less visible acts of *pleasure*: filming female and LGBTQ-friendly porn, going to masturbation workshops and getting herbal yoni steams and massages (more on what those are later). Some women looking for casual sex are skipping the dick-pic minefield that is Tinder in favour of the safer, female-first playground of orgasmic meditation or building their own dating apps like Bumble, where female users have more control.

Once I discovered a little of this, the rest of it unravelled like a secret girls-only network: every person I spoke to told me about some book I must read or some tantrika I should interview. This isn't *Fifty Shades* – these are practices explicitly touted as *good* for women rather than just interesting to them, often carrying the claim of being healing rather than just X-rated. (By the way, even that BDSM bestseller has its own feminist rewrite, *How Not to Fall*, by none other than sexologist and educator Emily Nagoski under her *nom de porn* Emily Foster. Her 'sex-positive, science-driven' novel, due out in 2016, will correct *Fifty Shades*'s damaging myths about female desire while keeping the erotic heat high.)

Sex survey data have only begun to hint at how women's approach to sex might be changing, but research suggests the group now most likely to be pushing the boundaries of sexual orientation and exploration is young women. Britain's 2013 National Survey of Sexual Attitudes and Lifestyles – one of the most comprehensive studies measuring how sexual behaviour and attitudes have changed over time, with 15,152 participants of all ages in its most recent iteration – showed the total number of sexual partners reported by women over their lifetime has gone up since 2000, the last time the survey was done, as has the number of women who have had a female partner, and the number who have had sexual experiences with other women (11.5 percent). Meanwhile, men's total number of female sexual partners has stayed flat in the same period, as have the numbers of men who have had same-sex experiences (8 percent). Participants reporting having had vaginal sex in the past four weeks actually *decreased* over the past decade. And age substantially affected women's responses. The number of women identifying as bisexual was highest in the sixteen to twenty-four age group – 2.5 percent compared to 1.4 percent of women of all ages – though that's far lower than the proportion of young women having woman-on-woman sex: over 18 percent of women thirty-five and younger say they've had experiences with the same sex, and about 8 percent have had same-sex experiences with genital contact. The answer to the question *What do women want?* is changing fast.

'The proportion of women reporting sexual experience with same-sex partners now exceeds that of men, at least at younger ages, when the proportion describing themselves as bisexual is highest,' said the study (which unfortunately didn't appear to track transgender participants). This may also reflect a greater openness among women in discussing sex with researchers.

These shifts are beginning to emerge in the mainstream conversation, whether it's Amy Schumer's raunchy talk about her clit or or a mega-hit song by an ostensibly 'straight' performer like Katy Perry about kissing girls and liking it. Like all good entertainers, they sense these statements will land because they're already lurking in the zeitgeist. In spring 2016, orgasmic meditation was featured in Gwyneth Paltrow's Goop newsletter. Sex that is initiated and driven by women is getting more visible; could it be long before Oprah is hyping clit-stroking?

This is the wild frontier of women's sexuality. Not all of it is for everyone, that's for sure; some practices are New Age–reverent, while some is decidedly, hilariously irreverent. It is vibrant and strange, riotous and messy, and as varied as women themselves. It turns out our culture's idea of average female sexuality is hiding a hell of a lot of nonconformity and experimentation. A lot of *play*.

'We're going to do a quick exercise,' says Rachel. 'I want every-one to turn to a neighbour, and when I say go, the person with the shorter hair is going to say, "What is your desire?" and the person with the longer hair is going to say their desire. Then repeat.' Rachel and Keenan demonstrate the game. Games like this, geared to engineer a sense of intimacy, are central to OneTaste's recruiting events, as I learn later when I visit their headquarters in San Francisco.

Each sweaty, half-naked person in the dome turns to the sweaty, half-naked person beside him or her and begins comparing hair lengths. A murmur arises, like the collective chattering that begins after the end of a school assembly.

A guy in his fifties or sixties with a thick Russian accent turns to me. 'You heff a long hair.'

'Yes, I do.'

'So vat is your desire?'

I feel the dirt caked behind my knees, in the folds of the elaborate bandage around my thumb where I sliced into it while cooking at my base camp last night. 'To take a shower.'

'Vat else?'

'To learn more about orgasmic meditation.' *Nice one, nerd!*

'Vat is your desire?'

'To dance at Robot Heart.' Boilerplate Burning Man response: Robot Heart is a very huge, very douchebaggy dance party.

'Goot for you. Vat else?'

To end this conversation. I could feel myself shrinking at the enforced sharing. 'To understand the nature of female sexuality.'

'Vell, look inside yourself.'

'I'm not every woman.'

At this, he becomes philosophical. 'None of us is every man or every woman. Vat works for one doesn't work for the other.'

'That's right. All right, your turn.'

'To get a good night's sleep.'

'That's not going to be easy here. What's another desire?' I say, sounding less than interested in his answer.

'To get a nice dinner tonight. Maybe learn something that I can please my wife.' He's been with his wife for fourteen years, he says; his daughter brought them both here. I smile.

Rachel is back on the mic, explaining more exercises. They seem designed to delay the gratification everyone's waiting for: watching a woman get off.

'Everybody, stroke your eyelid. That's how light you're going to stroke her. That light, slow stroke. Does anyone want to know why we start with the woman? What is the technology that most women use to get off in the world?'

'Men!' calls out a man.

'The vibrator, right?' says Rachel, to much laughter. 'And what is the technology most men use to get off? The *internet*, right? So, what's going on here? What's happening is women have very easy access to a partner. She could walk ten feet out onto the playa and get fucked very easily. But women have difficult access to what we call "direct orgasm." So they can have sex, but it's often not very satisfying! That's why they use the vibrator. Men have very easy access to direct orgasm. They can use their hand, they can get off – it's simple. But it's difficult for men to have access to "empathetic orgasm." They're not taught how to *feel* their partner.

'It's actually pretty radical. Because she actually gets to feel without *owing* anything. He gets to practice having the amount of skill of playing her body like an instrument, and intuiting what she wants before she asks.'

'Does the woman *ever* please the man?' shouts someone.

'We do have a practice of male-stroking. It happens three years in.'

Gasps and murmurs of astonishment erupt.

'After three years of dedicated pussy-stroking! After you've lain on your back for *three years*!' Rachel looks about, triumphantly registering her effect. 'It's after a woman gets *so*

full and so fat with orgasm, that she can stroke his cock and have it feel good to *her*.'

The crowd processes their reactions to this. In a world where most of the sexy techniques vaunted in manuals and women's magazines are still meant to *please him* or *drive him wild*, one that explicitly ignores the penis altogether has the ability to surprise, even unsettle, people. *It's easy to make a penis happy* seems to be the message. *Let's focus on the area where we need remedial education.*

To everyone's bemusement, Rachel wants us to do another exercise. I pair again with Old Russian Dad. I feel uncomfortable.

A young man sitting near me mumbles his impatience with listening to this whole spiel, loudly enough that others can hear. 'Just cut to the chase. Tell us what to do. Like, there's a lot of people here.'

A girl sitting next to him answers softly. 'I think they're trying to convey the *values* of it. It's not *just* the ...'

Keenan describes the next exercise, but Old Russian Dad can't hear, so I repeat. 'First, touch my arm in a way that you think will feel good to me. Probably not sexually, necessarily,' I add. He does. 'Thanks,' I say. We both laugh, nervously.

'Now, stroke your partner's arm like you're trying to make *yourself* feel good,' says Keenan. 'In the same way you'd touch nice fabric or your pet to make yourself feel good.'

Old Russian Dad does so, further up my arm.

'All right,' I say. 'Thanks.' I've had enough of this. I'm a relatively open-minded libertine, yet all the naked people at Burning Man haven't made me feel as jumpy as all this ... *intimacy*. What does that say about me? I resist the impulse to fall stone-silent and so I tell ORD my name. His is Alex. I suddenly feel empathetic: he's probably more uncomfortable than I am.

Meanwhile, Rachel is charging full steam ahead with a generalization-packed analysis of gender differences in the bedroom. He be like *this*, but she be like *that*. She's like a comedian in a Manhattan basement club, and the room is eating out of her hands, impatient for the big payoff.

'The stroker isn't going to ask the strokee, *Does this feel good to you?* 'Cause she'll *lie*.'

'A*h, word!*' says a woman near me, the same woman who has sucked too many cocks that she didn't want to suck.

'The desire to know if it feels good for them is that ego thing,' says Rachel. 'But what we find is if we're stroking for our own pleasure, it does actually feel best to her. And learning to use your body as your compass is one of the …'

House music continues its hypnotic thumpy-thump in the distance. *Bootsandpantsandbootsandpants.* People are zoning out.

Thankfully, there is an audience question. 'Is it common for a *man* to climax while doing an OM?'

'It's not common, but it's possible,' answers Rachel. People near me perk up.

'It's possible for the stroker to feel an "empathetic orgasm,"' says Keenan. 'Because we as people *feel* each other. If something happens in there, I feel it. If there's a woman orgasming next to you, you're going to feel it.'

The concept of having a mini-orgasm caused by the person next to you having an even bigger one seems to confuse and fascinate everyone. If that's true, what's going to happen when a woman has an orgasm in front of us in just moments?

'So, guys, just so you know, I stroke as well,' says Rachel. 'It can be done in any gender modality, but we recommend you start with a man stroking a woman.'

I guess lesbians just are going to have to break the rules and recommendations, as always. A huge blind spot in the OM philosophy is its heteronormativity – its continual references to a man stroking a woman as the default, and defence of those norms when challenged. It's also a common wider criticism of some forms of tantra and spiritual sexuality – that because of their worship of the balance between the 'goddess feminine' and 'divine masculine,' they tend to address homosexual pairings as an afterthought, and transgender and genderqueer people rarely if at all.

'So in the demo we're going to do in a little bit –' (sighs of relief) '– you're going to feel how it feels to be in the field of a woman in orgasm. You'll feel it in your body. When you stroke, later, if you decide to do so, you'll be stroking because *you* feel good in your body. Her enjoyment is a *by-product*.'

I can't see very well from my spot at the back, but there are rustlings up front. Chairs are being moved around and pillows arranged. A woman I hadn't noticed until now is shuffling around, talking with Keenan.

'You stroke with gloves, especially on the playa, 'cause it's gross out here...'

Old Russian Dad whispers to me that all this happened before, at end of nineteenth century, in medicine. Female patients suffering from 'hysteria' would be stroked by their doctors. It's all happened before, he says. I nod.

'We're about to do this demo! You guys ready to see this demo?'

There are *woo*s, though people are either being very polite or everyone's holding their breath. The macho contingent isn't high. Dudebros who are just here to see a naked lady wouldn't sit through an hour-plus presentation about feelings.

Cross-legged on mats on the flat desert ground, people strain to see over one another.

'This is a very vulnerable position for Natalie to be in,' says Rachel. 'So it doesn't matter if you can see or not. It doesn't matter because it's all about this *feeling* and the sensation that's going to be transmitted. So we're creating a little energetic bubble that she is going to *fill* with her orgasm. And you're all going to be able to feel it. That being said, one of the ways that we create the bubble is by people sharing "frames" during their experience. Now, a frame is a moment of sensation in your body. *I feel heat in my chest, I feel sensation in my face, I feel sweat on my left arm*. It's a moment of sensation. One of the ways to stay present during a demo is to call them out. So why don't you guys practice a little bit, popcorn-style, calling it out?'

'Heat on my neck,' says a guy.

Everyone begins murmuring.

'Tightness behind my eyes,' says a man.

'You guys are great at this! Pros! So you're going to keep doing that as the demo goes. We're going to get set up now.'

'During the practice, there are a couple of touch communications that might happen,' says Keenan. 'Natalie might make requests, very specific. "Could you stroke a little faster, a little harder?"'

Rachel: 'Everyone take a deep breath!'

The sound of breath.

'Salivating,' calls a guy.

The woman who had been sitting silently behind Rachel and Keenan during the presentation now lies down and, I assume, takes off her pants and lets her legs fall open. I assume this because I can't actually see anything beyond Keenan's head and shoulders. Neither can the people around me. People lean in, but surprisingly, no one stands or jockeys for a better spot. In this free city where people act on their wildest desires, what everyone wants now is to stay respectfully seated, even if they can't see the mostly naked woman. I do notice figures behind us leaning against the dome's exterior, looking in.

'I'm going to do a little anatomy before we start.' Keenan slips on rubber gloves, puts a dollop of lube on his finger. 'Starting down here is her anus. That's called the introitus. The section between her anus and introitus is the perineum. Up here are the outer lips. Right? We spread them open, you can see her inner lips. The inner lips, or the inner labia, come up and they meet to form the clitoral hood, and under that clitoral hood …'

The atmosphere is charged with tension. *That* I feel in my body. I've heard little about OM or OneTaste at this point, but later I'll read about other OM presentations that take place in halls and on stages, rather than in the middle of a punishing desert so arid that it has neither insects nor scrub, just flat, open nothingness, miles from civilization. At these other presentations, the half-naked woman is always up on a gently lit platform, flanked by friends and OM people; there are exits and entrances; there is carpeting and coffee and muffins in an anteroom. Here, this woman named Natalie is lying on a couple of layers of filthy mat and carpet on the bare, brown earth, separated from hundreds of dirt-smeared strangers by little more than a couple of metres, accompanied by just a handful of her associates, at a massive party whose selling point has always been its lack of rules, its tumult and its anarchy – a place where you may do what thou wilt, and that shalt be the whole of the law.

At other times, other places, in other cultures and contexts, this scene, a half-naked woman on the ground, her legs spread, a man who is not her husband bent over her, a leering mass of grimy strangers crowding around them – in other places, this scene can't be anything but one of horror and nightmare and tragedy. This woman on the ground, this woman named Natalie – she has serious balls. Unimaginably gigantic ovaries.

'… is her clitoris. All right? And I'm going to be stroking the upper left-hand quadrant of her clitoris, basically the one o'clock spot on her clit. Under the hood, directly on her clit.'

Silence as she is stroked, except for the distant *thumpy-thump* of the bass. On top of the sensation of danger, there is a strange clinical feel, thanks to Keenan's rubber gloves and his calm narration and the word *introitus*. It is as if we are in a grand sixteenth-century anatomy hall, and some starch-ruffed *professore* is pointing out the intimate bits of a hired, bored prostitute on a table. Or slicing open an unfortunate woman's corpse.

Really, though, the truth is that there is no existing comparison point, past or present, for the scene that is unfolding. All historical equivalents have been situations where the woman is decidedly not in power. Here is the same physical configuration, but the power positions have been reversed. The woman on the ground is the object of our attention, yet she's also the individual calling the shots, instructing *more* or *less*; the recipient of pleasure rather than the giver of it. The effect of this is absolutely electrifying.

'You can see some of the signs of orgasm already,' says Keenan. 'You can see her toes are pointing a little bit.'

'What?' people call restlessly. 'Louder!'

'So, I encourage you guys to just feel your bodies right now,' calls Rachel. 'Worry less about the details. We'll answer all your questions after.

'Now I'm touching her directly on her clit.'

And then we hear it, a low *uhhhhhhhhhh*.

Uhhh, uhhh. Ah.

Suddenly a guy calls out. 'Tension in my jaw muscles.'

'Tension in my chest,' calls a woman.

'Tightness in my belly,' says another woman.

Oooohhh ohhhh, ohhhhhhh ohhhhh OHHHHH ohhhh, OHHH ohhhh. Ohh ohh ohhh ohhhhhh.

'My belly is inflating,' says a woman.

'I feel tingly all over my body!' says another woman.

'Me too! says another.

The moans are now impossible not to hear, even for us in the back.

'My heart's beating really fast,' says a guy.

'There's a ball in the base of my throat,' says a man.

Haaaahh, huuuhhhhh.

'I'm breathing slower and deeper,' says a woman.

'I feel like I'm falling forward,' says a man.

'I'm feeling lightheaded,' says a woman.

Uhhhhhhhhhhhhhhhhhhhhhhhhhhhhhhhhhhhhhhhhhhhhhhhh-hhhhhhhhhhhh.

Thump thump thump thump thump goes the distant bass.

HUHHHHHHHHHHHHHHHHHHAAAAAAHHHHHHHH-HHHHHUHUHUHUH HUH HUH HUH AH AH OH OH OH OH OHHH OHHH OHHHH!

Her moans rise in pitch.

OH OH OH OHH OHH OH! OH! OH! OH! OH! OH! OHH! OHHH! OH! Ohhhhhhhh huh huh ... HAAAAAAAAUUUUUH-HHUHHHHHUHHHHHHHAAAAAHHHUH HUH HUH HAH HAHAaaaaaaahhhhhhhhhhhhh.

Natalie has just had an orgasm – sorry, a *climax*. Nobody asks whether she has or not. She has.

People laugh and sigh.

Ahhhh ahhh ohhhhh ohhhhhh ohhhhhhhh ahhhhhhhhhhhh-hhhhhhhhhhhhhh Ah! Huh, huh, huh, oh, oh.

'I feel my heart expanding,' says a woman.

'My heart is racing,' says another woman.

'My chest is full,' says a man.

More laughter.

'I feel I'm in a trance,' says a woman.

'I wish I could see,' says another woman.

Natalie is still moaning, but it's softer now. Then it rises again with staccato *uh*s and *oh*s. She may be having a second, or third. Her noises rise in pitch and intensity.

'I feel very happy!' calls a woman.

Ohhhhhhhhhhhhhhhhhhhhhhhuhhhhhhhhuhhuhhhhhhhhhhhh.

'My knees are wobbly,' says a guy.

'I feel like crying,' says a woman.

'Forgot to breathe,' says a guy.

'I'm feeling jealous,' says a woman.

'I'm feeling jealous,' says a guy.

Giggling and relaxed laughter.

'Feeling high,' says a guy.

'Feeling relieved,' says a woman. 'My body feels so relaxed.'

'I feel inspired,' says a guy.

'This is the last two minutes of the OM,' says Rachel. 'He's going to bring her down, so she isn't walking into walls afterwards. He's doing firmer strokes in a downward motion to bring her down. He's going to give her some grounding pressure. He's putting a lot of pressure on her pussy to push the blood back into her body from her engorged genitals. It's so that you can walk around, go grocery shopping, without feeling like an insane person.'

'There's a deep feeling in my anus!' calls out a guy.

Natalie sort of moan-laughs in relief and elation. She sets off sympathetic noise in the crowd. Applause erupts. Woos. Cheers. Sustained cheers and applause.

The whole practice has taken just ten minutes.

'Now they're both going to share a frame,' says Rachel.

'There was this moment when I felt a vibration in my undercock that went up my scrotum,' says Keenan.

Natalie, for her first and only remark, lets loose a positively Joycean stream of consciousness. 'There was this moment when there was this tight ball of burning and tingling *ch'i* in the centre of my clitoris and I felt all at once push out all the way down in these waves of tingles all the way down my legs and all the way down my arms.'

'Thank you, Natalie.'

'Thank you, Natalie!' everyone calls.

What we are witnessing is both completely real and genuine, and also a perfect act of show business. I feel like I'm in a Baptist church hearing a marketing pitch from Pussy Jesus.

'So, that is a demonstration of what's possible. Both of these people have been OMing for about five years. So don't think your first OM is going to look like *that*, folks! Like when you see the yogi master do the headstand. You're going to go back and learn scales, and that was like a concert. Get it? So if you think you actually want to do this practice, if you think you wanna OM at Burning Man, the group practice is here, at 6 p.m., and 9:30 a.m., in the orgasm dome behind us. You will get walked through the whole thing by our own instructors. Bring a partner. Find somebody on the playa. Men are like puppies. They just want to please you. We've already had two hundred people go through this on the playa. We'll have two hundred more!'

Women put up their hands: could any of OneTaste's practitioners partner with them? No, they are told. Part of the practice is finding a partner and asking for an OM. Later, a rep quietly explains to me that OneTaste could be nailed for prostitution if they supplied paying women with sex partners.

That's when Rachel closes in on the sale, the reason to give OneTaste your money. 'You are now OM-trained on the playa. You're *not* OM-trained in the world when you leave here. This is a perfunctory training you guys have just gotten that is good for Burning Man, but if you think you want to bring this practice into your bigger life, make sure we have your email address and your phone number, and we'll call you. We have communities all over the world ...'

The crowd is full of women and men who are ready to give out their email, credit card, whatever is necessary.

'What are you leaving with here today?' Rachel asks.

People in the crowd call it out.

'Good ideas!'

'Love!'

'Inspiration!'

'Community!'

'Energy!'

'It is a golden age of women's sexuality in this moment,' says Isis Phoenix (her legal name), a Massachusetts teacher of sacred sexuality. She is one of many young women who have had an idiosyncratic journey of sexual discovery – except she has turned it into a career. She's now finding the world knocking at her door.

It may be hard to wrap one's brain around this idea. A 'golden age of women's sexuality' at a time when sexual violence is still rife, a time of 'slut shaming' and rape culture and Gamergate and the Jian Ghomeshi trial, when women who express opinions online are targeted with murder and rape threats, when mainstream porn demeans and subjugates its poorly paid actresses? Indeed, what we are seeing is two tendencies at the same time. The world, even in the West in 2016, is still not safe enough for women who wish to express themselves, and even less safe for women of colour, women of size, women who are transgender. This shouldn't be minimized.

But under the radar, some young women's sexual openness and experimentation are growing. Not the no-strings hookups and frat drink-a-thons hyped in the media that have parents scared, but more sober and considered experimentation (well, maybe after a joint). Rather than teens, these tend to be women in their late twenties and older, closer to what is thought to be the late-thirties female sexual peak. Their self-confidence is higher. They care less about what others think. Most of planet earth pays little attention to their sexplorations, and that suits many seekers fine – more can be dared *sub rosa*.[10] But wherever there is a safe space, at a festival or in a private living room, you may find women boldly going, asking, trying, playing. They may not know exactly what they're looking for yet, but like Georgia O'Keeffe, they sense that mystery, that 'something unexplored about women that only a woman can explore.'

Phoenix is one of them. In fundamentalist Bible belt Oklahoma where she grew up, she says, women's sexuality was not particularly celebrated. 'There was a hunger inside of me,' she says. One day a college professor introduced her to the town witch. Yes, a witch – a local writer who was into female divinity, the ways menstrual cycles connected women to the moon, how different herbs healed the womb. All of this piqued Phoenix's curiosity. She got into naked yoga, another practice exploding in popularity among young women. But when she wanted to teach naked yoga, her mother said, *No way.*

'My mom said, "If you're going to do anything like that, you need to change your name,"' she says. So she did. Melissa from Oklahoma became Isis Phoenix of New York City, then Massachusetts and finally Portland, Oregon, now in her mid-thirties. She styles herself as a 'sensual shaman,' offering services to women that intertwine healing and sexual awakening. With a constellation of herbs from her garden such as *artemesia vulgaris*, or mugwort, long used in traditional medicine to cure irregular menstrual cycles (to 'activate the womb's intelligence,' she says), she does ninety-minute customized treatments that could include a yoni steam, in which vulval tissues are exposed to gentle, herbal mist (not to be tried at home, mind you, unless you want a burned yoni). If desired, she'll do a yoni massage, where sensitive points in the vulva are stroked to relax, promote sensitivity to pleasure and even heal deep effects of past trauma (the two are often linked, since mentally detaching from one's own body is a key coping mechanism for sexual-assault survivors).

'In women who see me, there may have been violations in the past, or just desensitization,' she says. 'They'll say, "I don't know what I want, because I can't feel anything."'

Phoenix may work with a woman's voice, doing exercises to help her ask for what she wants, explain techniques to extend her orgasms or teach her which sex positions are best for specific issues. She'll have her walk barefoot in the grass, to feel more connected to the earth. It's all done in a carefully lit space calibrated to feel comforting, in which the woman hears repeatedly that her vulva is sacred. Women often buy four visits in advance for $160 each. We may scoff at such unscientific treatments, but if customers leave feeling healed, newly confident and sexually reawakened – especially abuse survivors, who may be allowing intimate touch for the first time in decades – for a few hundred bucks rather than the thousands demanded by doctor or therapist visits, it's hard to find grounds on which to object. Yoni massages and steams are increasingly available in Toronto, New York, San Francisco and other cities around the world, if you know where to look.

I'd known it existed in Toronto for months by the time I worked up the chutzpah to try it myself.

I like to consider myself open to new things. I've tried orgasmic meditation (verdict: even though it's not goal-oriented, it's effective at reaching goals) and a few other adventurous practices with my partner. Yet the idea of a strange lady's gloved fingers all up in my jade palace falls somewhat outside my personal boundaries. I'm bisexual, so it's not the 'lady' part, it's the 'stranger' part. There is some knowledge that can't be gained through interviews, however – Carlos Castaneda wrote something to that effect. In his case, his experience involved getting high as fuck on peyote; mine was going to be a spiritually enlightened pussy massage.

Viktoria Kalenteris is a sex coach, body worker and self-described 'zen kinkster' versed in both Taoist spiritual sexuality and BDSM. She is the founder of Playful Loving, offering classes and coaching out of a Bloorcourt upstairs workshop, in the west end of Toronto. She has an Etobicoke home studio for her yoni massages, which are part of her full-body chi kung massage treatments. She draws from Chinese holistic medicine as well as tantra for the massage, which aims to balance the body's qi, or energy flow, and that includes breasts, belly, vulva and vagina – areas strictly off-limits to traditional RMTs, for good reason: the average client would not take it well if a massage therapist offered to work out the kinks in her vag. But to Kalenteris, the body parts under the white towel are no less prone to pain, tension and traumatic injury than shoulders and knees – and just as responsive to healing touch.

She recently had a fifty-two-year-old client with vaginismus, a condition where the vagina involuntarily closes tightly, often accompanied by pain. The condition – more prevalent than many realize – started after the client was sexually assaulted at age sixteen. She had been unable to approach sex all her life, to even look at her genitals. Traditional therapy hadn't helped. After a few gentle and gradual yoni massages, though, the client had a breakthrough.

'It was the first time she'd allowed a finger inside her without pain since she was sixteen,' says Kalenteris. 'She was crying.'

For some, the $170 to $200 treatment is a simple luxury, a hedonistic experience. But for others, it can bring up subconscious images and emotions. Some cry. Others let out a primal scream, or strings of F-words. Others laugh. Kalenteris believes touch can unlock and heal memory of traumatic events that are stored in the body's tissue itself. Experienced in a safe space, this revisiting can be deeply healing.

'What I tell people is, we're rebooting the body,' she says. 'We're building connections between body and mind.' She's careful to note this isn't appropriate for all assault survivors, and it must be approached with extreme caution to avoid re-traumatizing. Consent is given and renewed multiple times during the process.

At her gleamingly clean and well-appointed home, Kalenteris carefully went through everything that would happen on the table in the softly lit room. There would be a head-to-toe massage focusing on energy points before private areas were touched. I would be covered with a towel, only one of my bits exposed at a time. A singing bowl would be placed on my body for the purpose of sound therapy. Finally, Kalenteris would don latex gloves and, after asking again for consent, approach the sacred flower with a fingerful of organic coconut oil.

Part of my brain was wondering, *Is this sex work? Am I a john?*

As the session began, though, coherent questions ebbed away. The foot massage was tremendous. The breast work was much-needed, considering how much tension I have in my chest from hunching over a keyboard. In some ways, it was just like having a tight shoulder kneaded and released by an RMT. In other ways, of course, it really wasn't. Waves of deep relaxation spread through my body. I felt drunk. My autonomic nervous system melted into goo. Halfway through, I tossed off the towels because not being totally butt-naked felt confining.

Then the yoni massage began. Gradually, with the inner thighs and skin around the vulva. I was impressed by the myriad ways a vulva could be stroked, inventive touch that focused on just tickling the inside of the left labia, or trapping the clit between the fingers and squeezing, while the other hand lightly brushes over it. *Guh lalala fnuhh*, burbled what was left of my mind.

Kalenteris worked her way inside, slowly moving in a circle, pressing gently along the vaginal walls.

And suddenly, she was done. This truth dawned on me with a note of frustration. No, more than a note. I'm not sure if it came from me or from some thirsty, red-eyed crotch dragon living in my vagina that had been awakened from a deep slumber and was now disgruntled: *Have I just paid for an unfinished hand job?*

Mercifully, before I could concoct a sacred-sounding way to phrase a request for a happy ending, Kalenteris performed a 'grounding' move, pushing down on my pelvic bone with the heel of her hand, pressing the blood out of my yoni and rooting me to the table. *Phew*. The dragon retreated reluctantly into its lair.

I got dressed dizzily, in an altered consciousness. My body seemed to have grown larger, vibrating outside its normal outline. I asked Kalenteris the time. Two and a half hours had gone by. I stared in shock; it was supposed to be a ninety-minute treatment.

'I could tell you needed more work,' she said, smiling.

I still do, I thought. But a sense of calm satisfaction was growing.

No doubt aware of my state, she drove me to Kipling subway station like an old friend, or just less of a stranger. We hugged. I kind of loved this woman.

Riding the subway east, I felt powerfully hungry, like I could eat two steaks. Then I texted my partner.

The yoni had been undeniably sexual, but it had also felt like a normal massage. The thing about sex is that context is everything. Being on a table, Kalenteris wearing latex gloves – the experience was contained. Regular massages can often feel sexual, too, though we're not supposed to talk about it. Female RMTs are inured to male clients' erections, and many have stories of being asked for sex. And then there are the 'massage parlours' where happy endings are de rigueur – they're not going away anytime soon. So why not offer this service in a context that welcomes women? While Kalenteris doesn't make orgasm an explicit part of her treatment, others do. I can see either option interesting women who want to pamper themselves, to awaken dulled genital sensation, to learn new moves or even to heal trauma and sexual difficulties that aren't addressed through therapy that engages only the mind. I can also see this appealing to women who'd like to feel for an hour or two like goddesses whose bodies are temples and whose needs are paramount.

Kalenteris, Phoenix and others are among a growing sister-hood of sex therapists who are creatively muddying the boundaries between holistic therapy and what we think of as sex work. While she doesn't refer to her treatments as sex work, other therapists I spoke to offering similar treatments do, and there are others who would if there weren't legal repercussions. If a woman pays for a treatment that includes a genital massage, experiences a release of long-pent-up rage and cries like a baby in her masseuse's arms, does that mean she's hired a prostitute? Does it make a difference if she comes or not? Do we care? It's clear that if these treatments continue to spread, they will one day present some gloriously complicated questions for ill-prepared lawmakers, and likely provide grist for a misguided crusade by an appalled (and bewildered) conservative male politician or two.

Stay tuned: it's coming to a city council chamber near you.

The most recent great misunderstanding of female sexuality was sparked, ironically, by a drug for men. Viagra, Cialis and their like work on men by acting on two chemicals produced during sexual arousal that relax the smooth muscle of the blood vessels in the penis, causing the vessels to expand and fill with blood – resulting in an erection. The pills block the breakdown of these chemicals, keeping more of it in the system and prolonging the hard-on. Increased genital blood flow is also a key sign of female arousal. But sending more blood to the vagina doesn't do much to make the owner of the equipment *feel* more interested in sex. Other substances, such as dopamine, that are precursors to ejaculation in male rats have produced contradictory results in females, inhibiting how often they stand still and raise their rumps for coitus during mating season.

So when people asked Pfizer et al. when they were coming out with Viagra for women, it set off a multi-decade scramble. The documentary *Orgasm, Inc.* offers a highly recommended look at the crazy rush to come out with unproven, occasionally dangerous, chemicals and surgical procedures to alter the female body so it can be aroused more efficiently – with less time and effort expended by women or their partners. This is sex for a high-speed world, where no one has any time for anything and the idea of taking half an hour or longer for foreplay is too inconvenient. But other than the invention of the vibrator, efforts to hurry up the female system have fallen flat. Sex stubbornly remains something that affects more than just women's genitalia – it is a function of her mind, her emotions and her psychology.

The lack of a female Viagra has been framed by some as a feminist issue. Why are so many drugs available to treat sexual dysfunction in men, but not in women? Even the Score, an advocacy group partly funded by Sprout Pharmaceuticals, used this argument to pressure the U.S. Federal Drug Administration to approve their drug, flibanserin (brand name Addyi), in 2015.

'I doubt some little pill is going to cure everything,' says Dr. Lori Brotto, associate professor of gynecology at the University of British Columbia. 'I think having more options for women is better – as long as women are in a situation or context in which they feel they're able to make those decisions. That they're not being told that the medication is the only cure.'

As we've seen, curious women are searching out new 'cures' that don't call for pharmaceuticals. At a weekend tantric sex course held in the basement and big, green backyard of a beautiful Danforth-area home east of downtown Toronto, eight students in their late twenties to late forties learned to gaze into each other's eyes, looking for the spark of the divine. Lucy Becker, Toronto's grande dame of tantra, guided them in kind, measured tones.

'Don't flow energy through your eyes,' she instructed, youthfully stepping around her paired-up students in a tank top, bare feet and long, flowing skirt. 'Soften the eyes. Sense your partner with your heart, your whole being.' Neo-tantra, a Western sex philosophy that borrows liberally – most South Asian religious scholars would say 'inaccurately' – from ancient Indian spirituality, isn't a new phenomenon in North America. Becker has run her popular introductory weekend course for couples and singles for decades, teaching how to generate sexual energy through breathwork and how to activate the heart more in lovemaking. But in recent years she has seen the average age go down among her students, from fortysomething to thirtysomething. The kids want to connect.

One Toronto software developer was twenty-five when he first took Becker's course five years ago. He loved it so much he has since come back multiple times, and now helps as Becker's assistant. 'It helped me discover who I am as a man,' he says. 'It told me a lot about what women want, what's important to them in a relationship.'

Across town, sex shop Good For Her holds its daylong workshop for anorgasmic women. Midway through the workshop, store owner Carlyle Jansen turns out the lights and instructs us to close our eyes and breathe rhythmically. We take long breaths deep into our abdomens, then begin to breathe more quickly, audibly expelling breath like we are having birthing contractions. Shielded by the half-darkness, we begin to rock our pelvises back and forth in our chairs.

'If you feel called to do so, make some sounds,' says Jansen, who in 2015 published *Sex Yourself*, a masturbation manual for women. 'What kind of sounds do you want to make?'

Some remain silent, but others begin to moan softly – *huhh, hunhh*. For fifteen minutes or so, we moan ever louder and rock faster. After it is over, Jansen asks the group how they feel. Some women report having more energy. Although they had kept their hands at their sides and hadn't been told to fantasize, some say they felt pleasant sensations between their legs. When a participant asks what happened, Jansen says the exercise is called 'kundalini fire breath,' and is meant to stimulate pelvic energy. If she'd elaborated further, it would no doubt only have sparked more questions.

Kundalini is a kind of energy, thought in some Indian spiritual traditions to reside dormant at the base of the spine, coiled like a snake. If stimulated by meditation, yoga, sex or other practices, it can awaken, travelling up the spine to emerge from the crown of the head in a shower of new insights. Some Hindu sages have described this as Shakti, the universe's supreme creative power, travelling upward to join her consort, the unchanging god Shiva, who resides above the forehead. Known as a 'kundalini rising,' this has been characterized variously as incredibly destabilizing, enlightening and life-changing.

Rather rarefied stuff for a sex-toy store, it brings up an intriguing question. Ordinary women are searching for unconventional ways to feel more desire and enjoy sex, and some are finding this leads down a path informed by ancient, Eastern traditions (even if they're watered down to the point they might be unrecognizable to a South Asian adherent living five hundred years ago). Is sex now becoming another gateway drug to spirituality for Western, secular women, added to the contemporary pile: yoga, meditation, acupuncture, ayurvedic diets? If so, we may be in a more weirdly transformative moment than we realize.

'This idea of a sacred sexual practice of some kind, it seems like it's getting more and more acceptance,' says yoga and tantra teacher Dee Dussault. 'Now, post-seventies, we're kind of open to the New Age – "we" meaning average North American people who are not necessarily very religious or spiritual.'

Playful and irreverent, Dussault doesn't much care where the line is between improving her clients' health, awakening their Shakti and guiding them toward unbridled ecstasy. A Torontonian in her early thirties who studied sexuality at York University and now lives with her husband in San Francisco –

where organic kombucha workshops are as common as tech start-ups – she is the founder of Follow Your Bliss, which offers both women and men courses in traditional yoga, nude yoga and tantric yoga that is calibrated for sexual awakening. Never mind the old idea that medicine must be bitter to be good for you: Dussault believes bliss is a legit path to wellness. She is equally comfortable giving a yoga class in the Vulvatron – a Burning Man 2014 art car shaped like giant female genitalia (its disco ball was the clitoris, naturally) – as in a traditional studio.

She says she wasn't really 'a super-spiritual, New Age, chakra type of person' until she attended an extended-orgasm workshop in Toronto with legendary female-positive pornographer, artist and sex educator Annie Sprinkle. 'We did a kind of kundalini breathing thing with her,' says Dussault, 'and I had my first non-genital orgasm. We completely weren't touching genitals, just breathing and making sounds and focusing on our chakras. And it was this really long, ecstatic, like *Aieek! Eeek!* – just crazy sounds, and a crying experience. It was just nuts.' Sex became her window to the sacred.

Her practice is, not surprisingly, exploding. Her ads show her either posed nude in graceful dancer asanas or draped in loose fabrics and smiling as if caught in mid-laugh, exuding tanned chillness. One of her client testimonials: 'I wept. I was in the desert; her practice was water, clear, cool and infinite.'

Some of Dussault's workshops are born from her fertile imagination. One day in Pavones, Costa Rica, near the Panama border, she was hanging out in a backyard with five twentysomething women she'd met while travelling. She'd invited them to the home of a female acquaintance where she was staying, and the yard was sunny and filled with sculptures, including a tall, totem-pole-like structure in one corner. A light bulb went off, perhaps the same one that went off for educator Betty Dodson in the 1970s when she was looking for ways to kick her nude female empowerment meetings up a notch.

'I think I said something like, "Hey, do you guys want to all go masturbate by the totem pole?"' says Dussault.

One of her favourite words, seemingly describing a higher state of being to which a person, a hip movement or a feeling can rise, is *juicy*. That afternoon met her criteria. 'I've never done anything like that before,' she says. The group walked to the pole, took off their sarongs and lay down, heads at the centre, feet pointing out at the world. Someone passed around a jar of coconut oil ('It smelled unbelievable, so fresh'), and the ladies got straight to it. Dussault offered a few extemporaneous words of guidance, as if leading a meditation sit. '*The universe is here for your pleasure,*' she said. '*Imagine that the sound of the earth is here to turn you on. The moan of the woman beside you is here to turn you on.*' Eventually, though, she dropped the instruction.

'After I got into it sexually,' she says, 'I lost the facilitator hat and I put on the masturbation hat.' They couldn't see each other's nakedness, but they could hear it. 'We became a cacophony, an orchestra. I don't know if other women were staying on the exterior of their vaginas or if they were going deep into their G spots and fucking themselves.' It all came to an end after an hour, the women's moaning getting quieter 'until we were all meditating or breathing in the afterglow,' she says. 'I forget who got up and said, "Okay, it's time to eat."'

Hedonism isn't traditionally something we consider a teachable, like algebra. Don't boys have circle jerks all the time without having to watch instructional videos? But grown women are different. They need to hear someone say, *Here is permission to go nuts*. Dussault hopes to introduce a real class someday, just as Dodson had her masturbation meetings – except she'd approach it as a kind of yoga. She'd instruct participants to 'contract or press out through your pelvic floor, imagine swirling energy moving through your pelvis' – to stay conscious during every moment rather than be lost in abandon.

All this underlines an impossible-to-ignore perk of the female sexual brain – the general lack of anxiety or discomfort around other women's sexuality. Although straight women may not be particularly attracted to other women or want to have sex with them, they seem less likely than men to be bothered by the idea of being near another naked person of the same sex, or to talk about pleasure with them. It's even a turn-on for some to be around other women who are turned on, in the way being around people dancing makes you want to dance. Especially when no one's watching. 'I'm hetero for the most part,' Dussault says, but that afternoon in Pavones, 'I found it so free to not have that masculine sexuality around, to have to manage that.'

This is perhaps related to what researchers have observed about women's more plastic sexual orientation. 'Women's sexuality and sexual orientation are potentially fluid, changeable over time, and variable across social contexts,' wrote the University of California's Letitia Anne Peplau and Linda D. Garnets in their 2000 paper 'A New Paradigm for Understanding Women's Sexuality and Sexual Orientation.' They cited evidence that shows women's sexuality is less determined by biological factors and more by the connection they feel with individual partners and by social influences – and, they pointed out, this may also explain the converse, why women are so good at repressing their sexual impulses absent encouragement from their culture. This doesn't mean all women can simply choose their orientation, however. Psychologist Lisa M. Diamond's groundbreaking 2008 book, *Sexual Fluidity: Understanding Women's Love and Desire*, found that many women experience shifts in their sexual orientation as involuntary.

'When it comes to sex, all women are gay. Some men are holdouts,' Betty Dodson, who considers herself pansexual, once quipped to an interviewer. That goes a bit too far – plenty of 100 percent straight and 100 percent gay women exist, as well as homophobic women. But they are less numerous, and evidence shows that as queer, bi and gay lifestyles become more accepted, more women will accept and nurture previously ignored or silenced parts of themselves.

What does sexual play and empowerment look like for *all* women – specifically those who aren't white and middle-class?

Being white affords privileges even in non-mainstream spaces of revolt such as sexuality. Considering histories of conquest and enslavement, the exoticization and violation of colonized bodies, whether they are First Nations Canadians or African Americans, it is bound to be incredibly complex. 'The black feminist tradition has never completely bought into sex positivity as a means toward a political end,' summed up an illuminating 2015 essay on *New York* magazine's The Cut site by Rebecca Traister. 'Stereotypes of hypersexualization have always made it harder for black women to be believed as victims of sexual assault and also made it harder for them to engage in a sex-positive culture.' She quotes black feminist scholar bell hooks, who said in a May 2014 panel at the New School that it may be better not to be sexual at all in any situation 'where I'm being mistreated, where I have doubt' – which could of course describe a lot of sexual situations women find themselves in. 'Let me theorize that it may very well be that celibacy is the face of that liberatory sexuality,' hooks remarked.

It's a question that requires far more depth and attention than this little book can offer, and there are black and indigenous and other writers of colour who can do it much more justice than I can. There are voices out there, for instance, that are reclaiming stereotyped and sexually objectified aspects of black culture and drawing on them as sources of autonomous sexual power.

Fannie Sosa is an academic, artist and dancer born in Buenos Aires who is using internet video to take back a part of black culture that she argues has been co-opted: twerking. She says the dance, which emerged out of bounce culture in 1990s New Orleans, is related to fertility dances – such as belly dance – done by women in several world cultures. It isn't just about fertility, though – she says twerking is actually an effective ancient method of birth control. The hip movements of twerking can act as a contraceptive by not allowing a fertilized egg to nest in the wall of the uterus, a concept she explains in a video aptly entitled *Cosmic Ass*. This detail is nowhere to be found in the blandly sexualized version of twerk that's become a popular mainstream white meme, the parent-shocking trendy club move du jour. White women have taken it upon themselves to lecture the likes of Beyoncé that 'twerking is not feminism,' as singer Annie Lennox said in an NPR interview. 'It's not liberating, it's not empowering.' This is part of an old pattern where white women police what behaviour gets to be called feminist, which has often meant excluding women of colour as well as lesbians and trans women.

'Very often people who say that twerking and feminism don't go together don't know what twerking is,' Sosa says in *Cosmic Ass*. Twerk is a way for black and diasporic women to remember where they come from, she says. And in a culture that places too much value on the head and mind, it's a way of sending love to a denigrated zone of the female body, to 'connect what I call the "pretty neighbourhoods," which are the face and the ego part, to the ghetto of my body.' Her videos offer a range of smart and funny twerking lessons set to hip hop. She twerks on the street, on rooftops and superimposed on top of waterfalls and forests. Showing off stretchy, high-waisted shorts, a cut-off tee and combat boots, she instructs viewers to wear something comfortable and sexy.

'Bring one leg to the back, flexing your knees,' she says, bending over and letting her long dreadlocks touch the ground.

'Imagine you have a pencil hanging from your pussy. Draw circles on the floor.'

Sosa's videos turn on its head the notion that twerking is done to get men's attention. She explains that women can use the move as an educational tool, a way of rewriting assumptions through play and humour. She twerks in public – at a party, on the street – and gleefully starts arguments with anyone who takes it as a sexual invitation. A common reaction from guys will be to come up behind her and grind their pelvises against her, sometimes called a 'hut' move. 'If somebody does that, you just turn around and hump them!' she instructs, acting it out in the video. 'You use your phallus – you were using your yoni twerking and then you use your phallus. All of a sudden they're like, "Whoa whoa whoa, okay okay, sorry!" It's fun for me, it's fun for the people watching and it can even be fun for the person who did the hut technique in the first place. Therefore, I think the lesson is absorbed with less trauma.'

Twerking is being reclaimed in other ways, including at 'TwerkShops' at the legendary women-run electronic music festival Bass Coast in Merritt, British Columbia. Imagine a crowd of tattooed, badass women vibrating their butts in unison to bass-heavy dancehall music in a grassy forest: that was the scene at the festival in 2015. Get your tickets now, ladies.

'It really started as a personal quest,' says Jenny Ferry. The founder of Soul Sex, a workshop that she calls 'contemplative sex education for adults,' was once about as far away from that as she could get. Years ago, she was an academic who taught natural resources, policy and economics at the University of Arizona at Tucson, and she lived on campus. 'I lived entirely in my head,' she says. Then she gave birth to her daughter, a visceral experience that, she says, woke her up to the fact that she had a body. She had been outdoorsy as a child, and realized she had allowed that part of herself to fade. She also realized her relationship was abusive, so she decided to leave. Then she realized she needed something else.

'Six weeks after leaving,' she says, 'my sex woke up and was looking for the buffet.'

Where does a newly separated single mom go to get laid? Like many other women these days who feel a budding desire for sex but want something safer or more fulfilling than OkCupid, Ferry ended up at OneTaste. She studied with Nicole Daedone for ten months, and left feeling driven 'like a madman.' She designed Soul Sex, and in August 2012 presented a pilot version of it in Victoria, B.C. She travelled with it along the west coast, offering classes from Vancouver to L.A. A single mom, she bet it all on these workshops, invested all her money and time. Yet, although Ferry was a newbie with no name to speak of, Soul Sex was a sellout.

The former professor sees something grander in this than just girls getting off, however. She believes it has the potential to transform a culture that has enshrined the brain as the locus of our humanity, one that prizes information, knowledge and linear thinking above all else and is doing so with increasing technological speed. 'With the humanist movement, we became so science-oriented,' she says. 'We have a very psychologized culture. In this decapitation and disconnection from our bodies, we forgot what it means to be human.' She feels that women have censored or repressed their emotional sides in the fight to be seen as equal to men, to enter disciplines such as law, medicine and business that have been boys' clubs since their inception. This was all the more necessary considering that women were for centuries denigrated as the sex that was somehow more bodily, governed less by reason than by base emotions.

Lurking in the background of all the soul sex, this return to the earthy body, is the 1970s – kind of like a cool grandma who wears a lot of caftans and nods knowingly when you tell her you've taken your first mushroom trip. When I told a roomful of older Canadian female artists I was writing this book, they immediately wrote down the names of books I needed to read. A.S.A. Harrison was pressed into my hands. Someone mailed me a copy of *Bear* by Marian Engel, the 1976 magical realist classic novel of rugged, pine-scented Canadian sexuality in which a woman falls in love and has sex with a bear in the woods (hey, it won a Governor General's Literary Award). I wanted to speak to people who had seen the sex-positive feminism of that era. I deeply wished Harrison were still alive – she died tragically of cancer in 2013. There were a couple of characters on the U.S. west coast about whom I was most curious, though.

In the late seventies, the Morehouse commune in Lafayette, California, acquired two new members, Steve and Vera. Each had originally found their way to the sprawling, twenty-five-acre purple commune for different reasons – his marriage was failing and he needed a room; her marriage was failing and a friend told her to take a sex course there. The two ended up marrying and living for over a decade in the community of about one hundred and fifty.

Steve and Vera Bodansky ultimately authored the vividly titled *Extended Massive Orgasm* in 2000, which has today sold about 100,000 copies, and the couple estimates they've personally taught orgasmic techniques to a thousand or so students. They got their sex educations decades earlier at Morehouse, a community named for its ethos of having *more*. It was a grand time for utopian experiments. 'I wouldn't call it a paradise, but it was closer to paradise than society,' reminisces Steve Bodansky, now in his mid-sixties. Morehouse was known for its purple-painted cabins, its strangely luxurious tennis courts, its odd outdoor carpeting, its druggy inhabitants and its unconventional guru, Victor Baranco. He styled the commune as a college called More University, designed all its courses and ran it all as its 'big daddy.'

'He called himself a "thug Buddha,"' says Bodansky. 'He was a smash-and-grab kind of person. He'd take your money but he also had this "power of now" kind of philosophy. He had a clock with no numbers on it, and "NOW" instead of the numbers. It was always Now o'clock.'

A key piece of Baranco's philosophy of now was the female orgasm – how a woman's lover could use his fingers to extend that shuddering moment to twenty minutes, to an hour, to more. Baranco didn't claim total authorship for his techniques; he said, cryptically, that he had learned from a witch. The Bodanskys studied hard, got PhDs and became resident teachers in Morehouse's Sensuality Department. After they eventually left – disillusioned, Steve says, by the camp's squabbling politics – they developed their techniques into a book, with in-depth illustrations of proper finger position and a parade of happy-looking, hairy vulvas. They went on to teach others, he says, among them a group devoted to the female orgasm founded in 1992 called the Welcomed Consensus – and they in turn taught Nicole Daedone, who distilled the methods into what is now orgasmic meditation and the basis of her OneTaste empire. (Daedone writes in her 2011 book, *Slow Sex*, that she began learning about sexuality by taking a course in San Francisco, though she doesn't elaborate.)

While OM is, aside from advanced variations, very much focused on one fifteen-minute practice of stroking precisely on the left-hand, upper quadrant of the clitoris, the Bodanskys teach dozens of styles, positions and techniques involving lighter and harder strokes, knuckles and labia – and, of course, ways to push pleasure long past fifteen minutes. 'OM is a good opening act,' says Steve. They teach an advanced version of what is commonly referred to as 'edging': bringing a woman to the edge of climax, then pausing, then bringing her back up, then pausing. Repeat until she is in a surprisingly stable, heightened, intense, undulating state of ecstasy. This can end in a traditional climax or five, or there might never be a climax at all. Pleasure can rise and fall indefinitely, for hours.

Steve says Daedone has been great at making female pleasure approachable to the masses, and the whole reason OM feels safe to many women is its simple design, allowing them to know exactly what is about to happen and when it will be over. But Steve and Vera graduated from More University, man. They don't teach *less*.

'Everybody who has the desire and is willing,' Steve says, including men. 'A lot of it is dormant. The more you do it, the more you'll feel. We like training women, giving them that *Aha!* experience. It's fascinating to feel like you helped somebody in that area. It's a miracle – it's a mundane miracle.'

The Bodanskys' approach aside, the sixties, seventies and eighties counterculture also saw a lot of men touting techniques of pleasuring women that were plainly tools to get the women more interested in having intercourse – *The Game* for the gentler hippie generation. The current wave seems more about women teaching other women to enjoy sex, whether with men or without. There was something about many of yesteryear's male sex gurus that always seemed ultra-cheesy, no matter how well-intentioned they may have been. Female tantrikas and sexologists, for whatever reason, are less prone to appearing creepy, less like they might try to invite you to their nag champa–scented pad after class for some Thai stick and an oily massage. At least, it seems easier and less triggering for many female abuse survivors to learn from another woman about reawakening their pleasure. (Or from a couple – perhaps that's why Steve and Vera worked so well.) But many of these teachings are open to male participation. Most of the female experimenters seem to want, ideally, to change the way men approach sex, too; they don't want to go off to some private, no-boys-allowed sex island (though some, of course, want exactly that).

This may all sound like an extreme pastime for sex-obsessed people with a lot of time on their hands. That wouldn't be strictly wrong. ('I'm addicted to pussy,' says Bodansky.) But the idea of a non-goal-oriented approach to sex is supported by clinical evidence about the way women describe their own patterns of arousal. For decades, women who complained of low desire were diagnosed according to a standard picture of a 'normal' sexual encounter. According to Masters and Johnson, sex was thought to be a linear progression beginning with the feeling of desire, moving to arousal, then plateau and, finally, climax. From A to B, with some diverting scenery in between.

But Rosemary Basson, a doctor who is a professor of psychiatry and gynecology at the University of British Columbia, noticed her female patients rarely described desire this way. Apart from the first months or years of a relationship, it doesn't typically spring up unbidden, a spontaneous urge that needs to be quenched. That, she observed, is a more male model of desire. For women, sex is often not a line but a circle. It doesn't neatly begin with desire or end with a climax. Women decide to have sex for many reasons – 237 distinct reasons, in fact, according to research by Cindy Meston and David Buss at the University of Texas at Austin. From wanting to connect and feel closeness, to wanting a mood boost, to feeling physically cold and wanting to warm up, the reasons were not even all sexual. If an encounter starts and the physical stimulation feels good, then arousal and pleasure can follow. *Then*, after sex has already begun, they may feel desire – desire to continue. Finally, an encounter ends with 'satisfaction' – not necessarily with an orgasm, but maybe. Sexual satiety isn't always the goal, however, nor do women always begin at the same spot, which is why the path is circular. This model was reflected in the fifth edition of the *Diagnostic and Statistical Manual of Mental Disorders*, a vindication that a linear model unfairly results in many women being labelled sexually dysfunctional when, in fact, they're just being women.

This model may not look much like the sex drive we see in the movies – the irresistible hunger, the clothes-ripping lust. Journalist Daniel Bergner was faintly critical of this circular model in his 2013 book based on his article of the same name, *What Do Women Want?*, describing it as 'quaint and demure,' as if Basson and other therapists are somehow cheating women of their dirty minds, taming women who *want* to be bursting with desire. Yet female patients react with relief and recognition when they are shown the circle. They're grateful to find out that their experience of wanting sex for many reasons, not just bare lust, is *normal*. It is called 'responsive desire,' desire in response to arousal, and it's more common in women than 'spontaneous desire,' the kind that hits you out of nowhere when you see someone who's smoking hot. And it's definitely sexy to know you're not abnormal.

There is an intriguing suggestion, supported by research chronicled in Bergner's book (a stimulating if sometimes infuriating read), that women's desire is not naturally lukewarm, though. It is neutered by monogamy. Human women evolved to roam from partner to partner, the theory goes, having multiple children with multiple males to increase their offspring's genetic fitness, and therefore they are, like men, turned on by *newness* – new partner, new body, new dynamic. They're turned on by sensing the lust of new partners *for* them. That's why women in longer relationships don't feel as much spontaneous desire – because we've civilized lust out of our lives in exchange for stability and child-rearing assistance.

That may be true, but evolution isn't destiny. We choose the relationships we want, and many women choose monogamous partnerships. Women are feeling more and more empowered to skip monogamy and find new partners who stoke their desire, of course. Single women outnumber married women in the U.S., and many of them are beginning to own that unapologetically, since they enjoy plenty of advantages over women in long-term marriages. Polyamory is also becoming more accepted as a choice, which is a long-overdue development. Opting out of monogamy should be supported much more in our culture. For women who *wish* to be in monogamous, committed relationships, however – and many do – defining burning desire and hot, irresistible sex as the norm is likely setting them up for failure.

What if, instead of seeing women's lack of spontaneous desire as a problem and searching for pills or therapies that fix it, we experimented with the structure of sex, moving its goalposts and changing expectations? Steve and Vera (who is fourteen years his senior) have been married over thirty years, and he expertly pleasures her every day. He spoke to me of how lucky he is to be with her. Not that their unconventional relationship is something that could or should be copied, but what if instead of trying to help people in long-term relationships restore the irresistible, addictive fire of an affair, we nurtured comfort and connection – whether that's as classic as clothes-on cuddling or as adventurous as OMing?

These oases of openness and idea-sharing about sex are few and far between in a broader desert. In much of the world, it's important to remember that women's sexuality remains either ignored or debased. Today's names for the female genitalia ain't 'jade gate' or 'passion flower' – they're 'axe wound' and 'meat curtains.' The No. 1 most popular definition for 'pussy' on Urban Dictionary is 'the box a dick comes in.'

In many ways, it's difficult to see how we've progressed beyond the attitudes of centuries ago, when women's genitals whose appearance didn't fit the ideal of small, white and tucked out of sight were pathologized and sometimes physically cut to size. Today, hardcore porn is the main venue where people (including girls who haven't yet picked up a hand mirror) are introduced to their first vulva.

Porn accomplishes through aesthetics and body shaming what thousands of terrible nineteenth-century doctors never could: it has made countless ordinary women voluntarily seek out the knife themselves, paying out of pocket for their own mutilation – or getting their parents to.

That's because, increasingly, those women are teenagers whose genitals haven't even matured yet. There has been such a surge in the number of teens demanding cosmetic surgery to trim, reduce and shape their vulvas this year that the American College of Obstetricians and Gynecologists issued guidance to concerned doctors on how to reassure patients and encourage them to seek alternatives, including psychotherapy.

Labia reductions and clitoral-hood reductions would not be anywhere near as successful economically if not for the porn industry doing their advertising. A University of New Hampshire survey found nearly half of kids aged ten to seventeen had seen porn online in the past year. Mainstream porn typically features one kind of pussy: the kind that either naturally or through surgical alteration is petite, narrow, hairless, neat and symmetrical, with thin labia and a tiny or even invisible clitoris. It's typically white, and if it's not, its non-whiteness is its fetish category – e.g., Latina or Asian or ebony. The ideal is a prepubescent slit, a serviceable hole with minimal 'extra' skin on the outside – never mind that this 'extra' is packed with sensitive nerve endings, and that trimming it can deaden sensation. Women who have had their outer labia lovingly massaged will tell you it feels deliciously erotic, and it's the perfect foreplay move – it stimulates and awakens the clitoral structure beneath the surface without being as sensitive as the clit itself.

Once again, we expect young women to be orgasmic sex kittens while neglecting, even mutilating, the parts of them that are made for pleasure.

Thanks to porn, we've also learned to prioritize the visual sense over the other four senses in sex, so the erotic information gained through touch and taste drops in importance. We've done this so thoroughly that it might never occur to us that sex *isn't* a primarily visual act. If anything, it's mostly one of blind touch, of negotiating weight and posture, position and texture, dryness and moisture, convex and concave. It's the animal senses sharpening, eyes blurring and closing, calves tensing, chest expanding, blood roaring. Video hides what sex really is. It is *safe sex*, playing out in the controlled testing ground of the mind, not the unpredictable space between bodies. It's festooned with terms like *high-definition, amateur* and *hidden cam* that create verisimilitude and the illusion of immediacy. But it leaves both men and women ill-prepared to deal with real, vulnerable human beings, and to reveal and revel in their own imperfect bodies.

This isn't to say that smaller genitalia are somehow fake or bad, any more than petite, thin women are – simply that they are only one option out of many, not the standard to aspire to. But mainstream porn presents a narrow and impoverished vision of femaleness (and manhood as well). Just as women's bodies come in a plurality of shapes and sizes, the pussy has a plurality of shapes and colours and sizes, and – at the risk of coming off as a motivational speaker – they're all beautiful. How could they not be? They're asymmetrical and floral, fat and folded and furry and furrowed, pink on the inside and brown on the outside and edged with violet. They have protruding inner lips that rub against thighs. They have Madonna moles and birthing scars. They draw attention rather than hiding, as pudenda should.

Alternative porn that features women and pussies of many shapes, sizes and colours, much of it made by queer and trans female producers, is finally challenging this way of looking. There are also groups springing up dedicated to helping people of every body type be more comfortable in their own skins. One of them is run by queer porn producer Caitlin K. Roberts, a rising young creator in Toronto's alternative sex scene. In addition to making alternative porn at TheSpitMagazine.com, which she founded, she holds semi-regular meetups called Body Pride, where people strip naked and hang out in an accepting space. They're aimed at people who typically get left out of society's picture of which kinds of bodies are beautiful: people of size, people of colour, transgender people, gender non-binary folk, the queer community and people with disabilities. They're not strictly about sex – they're about self-love. At the end of some meetings, there's a triumphal photo session, all reinforcing the message *You look gorgeous.*

There is also a spiritual sex practice that has a different approach to body pride. It makes the idea of diverse genital shapes and sizes into a teaching. Quodoushka is a collection of sexuality practices that claims to draw its lineage from Native American and Mayan shamanism – a claim made by its part-Irish and part-Cherokee founder, Harley Reagan, which has been contentious.[11] Regardless of its origin, the most interesting part of Quodoushka is its genital zodiac. Just as astrologers believe your sun sign determines your personality, Quodoushka holds that everyone is born with a sexual type that corresponds to the shape of their vulva or penis. There are nine vulval types and nine penile types, whose specific physical characteristics are lovingly illustrated in a book, *The Sexual Practices of Quodoushka*, by Amara Charles.

For example, you could be a Buffalo Woman, with 'large, protruding, thick outer lips, which curl and hang downward in cascading layers of skin … many lovers enjoy sucking and tasting these sumptuous, earthy folds ...' Or a Wolf Woman, with butterfly-shaped labia; they 'love to moan and howl during sex.' Or a Coyote Man, with his shorter penis and emotionally sensitive heart. The book will tell you how long each vulva type takes to orgasm, the distance between the clitoris and vaginal opening for each, which positions they prefer and whether they're sexually cautious or free-spirited. If you have a spare afternoon, open the book, sit down with your sweetie, take off each other's pants and try to figure out which animal you are. It works best if you have a drink or two. (*I'm a Cat. You're a Deer. I think? Ew, are we having inter-species sex? Time for another drink.*)

I won't try to say this isn't bananas. (It's bananas.) But it's also another tool with the potential to heal women's rocky relationships with our bodies. Other books and art projects out there (such as *Femalia*, a 2011 volume of vulva photography edited by Joani Blank) have sought to present an array of real lady-bits to combat unrealistic pornographic imagery. But Quodoushka is the only one I know of to list the erotic benefits of having long, floppy labia, a generous vaginal opening or a fleshy hood that makes finding your clit a matter of detective work. None of it's abnormal – it means you're a Wolf Woman, a Dancer Woman, a Sheep Woman. It could only be improved by including intersex and trans genitalia, too.

Seeing the anatomy types can have a huge impact. One woman who took the course in Chicago was so affected when she saw her genital shape reflected in a drawing that she imme-diately cancelled a booking for cosmetic surgery on her asym-metrical labia, says Barbara Brachi, co-founder of Toronto's Institute of Contemporary Shamanic Studies, who teaches a Quodoushka course. Hearing you're normal is powerful. When I showed *The Sexual Practices of Quodoushka* to a female friend in her late forties, she said it was the first time she had seen her genitals accurately represented. She had always thought her vulva was misshapen and ugly, and was relieved to know she was perfectly normal for a Buffalo ('powerful sex drives … intuitive, giving lovers'). Strangely, her personality matched the Buffalo's, too. Who wouldn't want to be a buffalo?

There are few women who have to fight hateful representation of their bodies harder than trans women. When they're not being out-and-out vilified, they're being packaged and consumed in pornography made by and for cisgender men (funny how that works). 'Chicks with dicks,' 'shemales' and 'trannies' have been high-selling fetish categories for decades – despite most trans women finding these words offensive. These usually feature a fantasy: a perfectly made-up, feminine-looking woman with long hair, lacy lingerie and heels who doesn't threaten the viewer's identity as a straight man, but just happens to have a penis. Performers must ejaculate on demand, like cis male porn stars.

The problem, however, is that the male-to-female hormone therapy process often limits the ability to ejaculate. This means tubes, fake semen and sometimes even a hidden assistant are required to create the necessary cumshots. Even worse: because trans performers whose bodies are unable to 'perform' command lower wages, many trans actresses will cut their hormone medication before a shoot – even though constantly varying hormone levels can have a range of damaging health effects, including a higher risk of osteoporosis.

One trans woman who had had enough of acting in these videos decided the best way to fight back would be to make *better* porn. Accurate porn that would be part-documentary, that showed real trans bodies and catered to trans women's desires, not desires and projections *about* trans women. Author, filmmaker, sexuality expert and trans advocate Tobi Hill-Meyer is the Seattle-based director of 2010's *Doing It Ourselves: The Trans Women Porn Project*, winner of the Feminist Porn Award for Emerging Filmmaker of the Year, as well as follow-up projects *Doing It Again* and *Doing It Online*, which picked up another award. Her explicit short film *Money Shot Blues & How to Fake Ejaculation* has been a hit on the film festival circuit. In it, she re-enacts her grim experience in commercial porn with wry humour and reveals much about real trans sexuality – it educated me deeply about both. (Her comment that at a certain point in their transitions, trans women ejaculate 'about the same' as 'every other woman' was eye-opening.)

Hill-Meyer's own erotic films feature explicit sex, but also scenes where performers do something unheard of in porn: talk about what they want and don't want *first*. Because trans women vary highly in the kinds of sex they prefer depending on how they identify, where they are in their transition and other factors, there isn't a no-brainer default, the way vaginal sex is for cis straight couples. That means that trans women are adept at using creativity, communication and empathy as a kind of brilliant foreplay. They're upfront about how their history or even ethnic background might affect what they're bringing to the bedroom. A typical video description for a mainstream porn might read, 'Kim sucks and fucks her boss.' A description for one *Doing It Online* porn reads:

Anai has had several negative experiences hooking up with cis women and was noticeably nervous when paired with Valentine, a cis woman who's never had sex with a trans woman. By talking it out, sharing their anxieties, and detailed negotiation and check in throughout the scene, they are able to become comfortable with each other, get the support they need, and have a wonderful time.

This is a safe space in pornographic form, a way for trans women to see healthy images of themselves. It's hard to think of a better example of how porn could be socially progressive – an argument that normally tends to puzzle people. Here, representation is power. Showing non-exploitative sex and real pleasure that caters to people who are attacked, murdered and driven to suicide b*ecause of their gender identity and sexuality* is potent. (Her work is supported by ordinary folks through Patreon, dear readers.)

Many transgender advocates specifically steer clear of discussing sex at all, in part because transphobic individuals tend to focus obsessively and invasively on what trans people do in bed as 'evidence' against them, in much the same way as homophobes do. But Hill-Meyer takes the opposite stance:

> Because so much discrimination is based on stereotypes, assumptions and prejudices about trans sexuality, it's important for us to be able to challenge it on that level and not retreat from these conversations … If we don't have this conversation with each other, then we lose out. As an example, I did a screening of one of my films a couple of years ago down in the San Francisco Bay area, and someone who attended wrote a long email to me the next day … She had assumed it would be impossible to transition and come out and have a healthy sex life … She said watching my film was a sea change where she suddenly could envision having a healthy sexuality. She had just assumed it was not possible for people like us.

Hill-Meyer has been the target of abuse, much of it, sadly, from a group of anti-trans feminists eager to police who gets to be counted as a woman. Her work is a way of combatting such transphobia – and it's one reason she wrote about trans sexuality for a 2015 women's sex guide, *Girl Sex 101*.

'There's this idea that women's sexuality means cis women's sexuality,' she says. 'Trans women's sexuality is a part of women's sexuality.'

Some of the more New Age experiments have their critics. OneTaste has been called out, in part for its fees. It might be a simple fifteen-minute practice (and you can buy OneTaste founder Nicole Daedone's book, *Slow Sex*, for $17), but there is a rising scale of more involved products, classes and packages sold to students. At the top is an 'intensive' with Daedone that reportedly runs in the tens of thousands of dollars. According to a former high-ranked OneTaste member I spoke to on condition of anonymity, members are under heavy pressure to sell all the time. Viktoria Kalenteris says she feels the company is too proprietary with knowledge that should be widely accessible to women. (Perhaps in response to criticism, the company's website recently posted a new statement about its finances, saying it has shifted the way it sees money, capping staff salaries and making other changes to aim more at 'giving rather than keeping.')

Many OneTaste members also come to devote themselves to OM as a pseudo-religion, says the former leader. I could see that at a highly rehearsed recruitment event I attended in San Francisco, where amped-up young men cheered slogans and wore T-shirts that read 'POWERED BY ORGASM.'

Perhaps it's not surprising that today's era of sexploration has a few of its own dogmas – after all, the heady flower-child utopianism of the sixties and seventies had its fair share of cults. One thing may give us pause. Female pleasure alone, once it's seen as a socially desirable good, is enough to inspire huge followings to devote their time and part with their money. Most cults at least promise messianic redemption via alien starship; OneTaste just has the clitoris. Either humans don't need an excuse for rabid zealotry, or the uncaged female orgasm has mystical powers as potent as Scientology's thetans.

There are ways of expanding your orgasmic repertoire beyond joining a quasi-cult. Just ask my friend Veronica (not her real name). She could write a few books on adventure herself, and her chutzpah has made her unlikely to ever need much help when it comes to catching a man, enjoying sex – or anything in life, really. We stayed in the same camp at Burning Man in 2013, and she loves it so much she's returned each year. A high-powered professional who travels the world and works for a well-known media company, she was back on the playa in 2015, looking for new ways to push her personal boundaries. She'd already tried nudity in a public steam bath (fun) and getting into a dark box with openings through which strangers could stick their arms, groping whatever they can grab (strange). 'I also did this thing where a guy "played" my body to music,' she says.

That's when she and three female friends stumbled upon an unassuming place called Spanky's Wine Bar. A sign on a door said 'SYBARITE.'

'I walked in and was like, *whoa*, what the fuck did I sign up for?' Veronica recounts. What she saw in a small, private room was a sort of pommel horse cut in half, with steps leading up to it and a seat and a pair of handlebars on top. On that seat was a vibrating device the size of a plum, with a little rounded nub on the end. That was where ladies were invited to take a seat.

The catch (if you call it a catch) was that the contraption was controlled by a joystick, and the joystick was operated by the 'doctor.' The doctor was a husband and father of two in his forties (attractive enough, she says, but not her type) whose wife was staying at the same camp and approved of hubby's project. In accordance with the rules of Burning Man, which asks every one of its 70,000 attendees to bring or do or perform something as a gift for everyone else, this was his contribution.

'He didn't have a sexual vibe at all,' says Veronica. 'It was more like a nurse caring for you. He said that he specifically turns down any advances.'

The operator said he would talk or be quiet as she wished, touch the rider only if it helped her get off, and she could choose to be either naked or partly clothed. Veronica opted for no talking and no touching, but 'I went full nude, because why not?' Finally, the Sybarite had a safety feature: 'a horn to honk in case you get overwhelmed.' An old-timey bike horn.

Assured by a friend who had tried it that it was worth her while, Veronica mounted the pommel horse. 'So yeah,' she says, 'six orgasms in forty minutes. I had the weirdest orgasm – sometimes I get foot cramps, but this time I had hand cramping and my whole face went totally numb. It was like an orgasm from the waist up.' She didn't honk the horn. After twenty minutes, she and the doctor started talking and giggling.

'He said my giggles were so infectious and so much of why he does this.'

The four friends rode the contraption one after the other (sterilizing alcohol wipe and a new condom on the device in between each, naturally) and emerged from the trailer in shaky hazes of pleasure, walking funny and laughing hysterically. 'We all walked out with the greatest faces,' she says. 'I'd do it again in a heartbeat.' Did she really feel comfortable, though? As nice as the guy was, he was a heterosexual male. He must have been enjoying himself.

Veronica made it clear, though, that there was no way he was enjoying it as much as she was. 'I really, honestly believed him when he said it was all about bringing pleasure to women and returning the favour for being such wonderful creatures who bring life into the world,' she says. 'It sounds hippie-ish. But in the moment, it was earnest and lovely.'

Veronica is a heterosexual woman, but at that moment she felt no desire for any man. Just the desire to sit on the little plum with the condom on it. She didn't mind doctor-nurse-operator-dude, not in the slightest, but he wasn't a big part of her turn-on, either. It was the pure play of it all, the feeling of being in a fit, strong body, the sensation and numbness and strangeness and laughter and weird nerve jolts coursing through her.

There is a German word, *Funktionslust*, that has no equivalent in English. It means the pleasure of functioning, the enjoyment taken in performing something you do best, like a bird flying or an athlete scoring. On the Sybarite, Veronica had *Funktionslust*.

At the Sexual Health Laboratory at the University of British Columbia, far from the madding crowd of music festivals and yoga studios, Dr. Brotto is clinically testing her own method of sexual healing. She runs the largest lab in the country exclusively devoted to women's sexual health, training a lens on topics that often go understudied, such as asexuality, genital cosmetic surgery and the effect of cancer on sex. Along with Dr. Meredith L. Chivers at the Sage Sexuality and Gender Laboratory at Queen's University in Kingston and UBC postdoctoral fellow Dr. Laurel Paterson, Brotto is one of a groundbreaking group of pioneering Canadian researchers whose work is transforming received wisdom about female sexuality. Unlike researchers before them, these scientists and psychologists are putting something new at the centre of women's sexual health: pleasure.

Brotto's work fills a desperate need. It's easier for creative, open-minded younger folk already dyeing their armpit hair pink to experiment, traipse to Burning Man, ride the Vulvatron and discover their bodies. Not so much for women who would recoil at the idea of being diddled by a stranger at an OM class or of a 'shaman' poking around in her 'yoni' – which is, need we remind ourselves, most women. Can the majority of women benefit from any of this, beyond puzzling over it in a Goop newsletter?

Brotto believes they can. She has spent fifteen years designing and testing a holistic therapeutic approach for women with common complaints such as low desire, low arousal, difficulty with orgasm and pain during sex. One of her key tools is a rising buzzword in the world of wellness, but rare in sexual health – mindfulness. It has been called a catch-all salve for our scattered, multi-tasked state, but Brotto is one of the first to apply it seriously to women's sexual issues in a clinical setting.

She is currently about halfway into a five-year clinical study of six groups of women with sexual dysfunction who are taught mindfulness, funded with a grant from the Canadian Institutes of Health Research. Results from a 2013 pilot project show mindfulness boosts women's self-reported sexual sensations and arousal, even their ability to reach orgasm. The practice curbs distractions and negative thoughts during sex, common problems women face. In other words, it helps them be present – which might sound familiar to OM lovers. Brotto has seen mindfulness work so effectively at healing sexual issues, she's working on a self-help book that will share with a general audience the techniques she's refining.

The women in her study come from across southwestern B.C. They drive or ferry or bus themselves to their morning sessions at the Vancouver General Hospital in the Department of Obstetrics & Gynaecology, where Brotto's lab is based. Some are referred to her through sex clinics, and some contact her after seeing an ad. They're then randomly selected for either eight weeks of conventional, supportive sex therapy or for a group that supplements the conventional sex therapy with meditation. A *lot* of meditation. It was originally a four-week program, but Brotto says she expanded it when participants asked for more meditation instruction.

Participants are far from being adventurous tantra seekers. Some are married and some single, some have children, some are new immigrants. Amid the sex talk, they often discuss demanding jobs and busy schedules. But they are ready to devote sixteen hours, plus regular at-home practice and weekly homework assignments, to investigating why this area of their lives has shut down. Some say this is a part of themselves they've always wanted to address. Others are there, they say, because they haven't made love to their husbands in years and don't know why.

The idea of using mindfulness as a sexual aid may sound odd. After all, mindfulness is based on an early form of Buddhist meditation called *vipassana*, which originated among celibate monks in isolated, austere temples. Isn't its entire ethos *opposed* to enjoying sex? Not exactly. Mindfulness has been lauded for its ability to train people to disentangle the bare sensory fabric of everyday life (the breath, sights, sounds, feelings) from their reactions to them (judgments, opinions, wishes, regrets). This helps practitioners suffer less in the face of life's pain, fear, confusion and loss.

While that is its greatest selling point (along with an improved focus on your golf swing), many students also report another benefit: they enjoy pleasant experiences *more*. This can be explained if we leave sex aside for the moment and talk about something neutral, like chocolate. A meditator may experience more of the pleasure of eating a piece of chocolate because she's cultivating more sensory clarity – her experience has increased richness, like boosting the resolution on a television set. So she's fully tasting every drop of chocolate melting on her tongue. But let's say the chocolate-eater also has some bad feelings interfering with the chocolatey goodness: some faint guilt about her waistline. While she's trying to enjoy the experience, she's also *pushing it away*, just a tiny bit. Or perhaps she's wishing the experience were better, the chocolate of a finer quality – or wishing there were more chocolate, dreading the rapidly approaching end of the experience. This barely conscious, constant sensory *push and pull* on the present moment interferes big time with fulfillment, creating that familiar sense we've all had after we do something that was supposed to be fun: that it passed us by without us really enjoying it.

If the meditator can tune into the taste of the chocolate and say *Yes!* to every second of it rather than letting her inner reactions take over, the experience transforms. Disentangled from interference and distractions, pleasure is experienced more completely for what it is in the moment – the simple, fleeting sensation of it. Which is all we ever have anyway. Result: same chocolate, heightened pleasure.

Hence: sex.

There is perhaps no pleasurable experience that has the ability to inspire more aversion, guilt, mixed feelings and inner cross-talk than sex. This applies even more so to women, and psychologists are trying to work out why. Women are thought to be more sensitive to negative social and cultural messages – more susceptible to the idea that masturbating is wrong, or that men enjoy sex more than women, or to unrealistic ideals about what women's bodies should look like. For women suffering from sexual issues such as low arousal and desire, mindfulness may offer them a new way of tuning in and amplifying pleasurable feelings and satisfaction – and tuning out self-judgment, anxiety and expectations like so much radio static.

Getting there is slow-going, however, and it's not a home run for everyone. Brotto's participants have typically never encountered mindfulness before. It may look like a lot of sitting with your eyes closed, but meditating is work. Brotto, who trains in mindfulness-based stress reduction in order to run the groups, guides them in honing their attention on their breath. In twenty-minute chunks, they are taught to mentally scan themselves – slow, careful sweeps of the attention through the body. 'Focus on sensations in the toes of the left foot,' they're told. 'Then the ball of the foot, the heel, the arch of the foot.'

Many participants find it challenging, battling sleepiness and confusion. Why are they coming all this way to focus deeply on their ankles?

It is in their fourth session that many in the group have their big *aha* moments. They learn an exercise adapted from mindfulness author Jon Kabat-Zinn called the 'thoughtstream,' where they observe their own thoughts.

'Imagine sitting by the bank of a stream and watching thoughts go down the stream,' the group is instructed. They're told to watch their thoughts arise and pass. If they get caught up in a thought – 'sucked into the stream' – they should simply climb out and sit back on the 'bank.' Watching the images and words that pop into their minds with clear, gentle attention leads participants to realize their heads are full of chatter – not all of it positive. Much of it, in fact, is deeply self-critical. And when they apply it to sexual situations later on, they learn that self-criticism doesn't considerately switch itself off during lovemaking. It often gets louder. Much louder.

'For a lot of women, that's a transition point,' says Brotto.

This constant stream of thoughts is an obstacle to sex, especially if they're negative. *Do I look fat? Maybe we should turn the lights off. Why isn't this feeling good? I'm taking too long to get there. I should just tell him to finish. He must be bored. Why am I broken?*

'The physical changes in our body that go with those thoughts actually compete with sexual arousal,' she said to one group. 'It's on a different system, parasympathetic and sympathetic branches of our brain.' If women go too far into their thoughts during sex, it can lead to what Masters and Johnson called 'spectatoring' – watching sex happen to them rather than really participating in it.

'Their bodies are just kind of going through the motions and their minds are elsewhere,' says Brotto.

Later on, the group is assigned much more challenging homework than following their breath. Go home, take a mirror and look between your legs. *Really* look. Notice what you see – the colours, the textures. Notice, too, any negative reactions, judgmental thoughts – and accept *those* without judgment. It's difficult stuff. Some women come to the group saying they can't do the exercise – coming face-to-face with their genitals makes them feel like vomiting. They're gently encouraged to try it again – and to confront false beliefs that come up as they look, 'the negative self-talk that our culture and society has laid on us,' says Brotto. She works to help her subjects deconstruct these beliefs, even to appreciate the beauty of what they see.

Toward the end of the sessions, the group is given new homework: touch yourselves, either with a vibrating toy or without, and use your mindfulness skills to notice sensations and thoughts, whether good, bad or neutral. Masturbation sounds like it should be easy homework, but for the group, it's a heartbreaking challenge. It isn't fun. It's an uphill battle that leaves many participants in tears. It also leads to real breakthroughs, however, and the group format allows participants to support each other. Many group members stay in touch after the sessions are over.

There is evidence that mindfulness may aid sex in yet another way. It may boost something called 'concordance.' (Sit tight – this is about to get a little sciencey.) Research has shown that subjective arousal (how aroused you feel) doesn't always match up with genital arousal (an erection or vaginal wetness). Someone can feel very aroused but not have much of an erection or have little vaginal wetness; the reverse is also true. For some reason, there is a higher rate of nonconcordance between genital response and subjective arousal (i.e., the two don't quite match up) in women than in men.

One of the world's key researchers studying how concordance affects sexuality is Dr. Chivers. Even if you don't know the Queen's National Scholar's name, you've probably heard of her experiments, which have been covered in the *New York Times* and other international media so often over the last few years that they are becoming something of a new Canadian Heritage Minute. (That hasn't been at all easy for Chivers, who has had to deal with negative attention triggered by oversensationalized headlines about her work.)

Her most celebrated experiments involve a La-Z-Boy chair and porn. She asks straight and gay men and women to sit in the chair in her lab and rate how much a given pornographic film turns them on. Meanwhile, a little device measures how aroused their genitals are.[12] Then the two measures are compared. Chivers's carefully designed studies, as well as her 2010 meta-analysis of related studies, have shown that heterosexual women have lower rates than any other group (homosexual women, homosexual men or heterosexual men) of concordance between the images that send blood flowing to their vaginas, which spurs vaginal lubrication, and the stuff they say turns them on. While they tend to get wet in response to a wide variety of images (gay male sex, lesbian sex, heterosexual sex and even bonobo monkeys getting it on), their subjective arousal is far more selective (films featuring heterosexual sex, especially those focused on female pleasure).

In other words, women can get wet when they don't *feel* at all horny. Or they can be horny and not at all wet. Both gay and straight men have higher concordance levels – their brains and their penises are more in sync, which won't come as a total surprise. Gay women, interestingly, tend to have slightly higher concordance than straight women, though not as high as men.

Chivers is extremely careful about not jumping to conclusions about the results – which is more than can be said of some crazed media reports that have appeared. *Women are lying about what turns them on! Women are freaks who are aroused by everything!!*

But the data is one thing; interpreting it is thornier. We can ask some reasonable questions. Do women not *know* when they're aroused? Or are their bodies aroused, but their minds aren't? On the one hand, this wouldn't necessarily be a problem. Arousal without wetness is why lube was invented. It's also why (despite the persistent myth that *if you're wet, you must want it*) vaginal wetness doesn't automatically mean a woman wants to have sex. As Emily Nagoski explains in *Come As You Are*, women will lubricate because they see something sexually relevant (*Look, it's sex*), but that doesn't mean it arouses them emotionally or psychologically. Humans also aren't built to have a 100 percent sync between our subjective feelings and our physical responses; men, with their wildly high concordance, may be a bit of an exception themselves.

The question remains, however, why this slight mind-body disjoint exists more in women (or, one might say, why it is absent in men). It could be the way women are wired from birth. But social factors may play a role. From a young age, girls are typically discouraged from becoming well-attuned to their genital arousal and desire. Added to this is the simple fact that girls' arousal is *harder to see*.

'How is it men appraise their emotional state about feeling aroused?' says Chivers. 'What are they taught is the strongest indicator of how they're feeling? The penis is their strongest indicator.'

Brotto echoes her thoughts. 'Boys, from a very young age, they receive feedback from their genitals,' she says, because they can see when they get an erection. 'They're in the bath, and the water is dripping on their penis, and they know it feels good. It's not in a sexual way, but they get that immediate feedback from the age of two and three. Women's genitals are hidden, number one, and number two, many of the messages women grow up with – *Don't touch, it's dirty, keep your hands to yourself* – may contribute to women being less aware.'

Because of this potent combo of negative social cues around their genitals, which girls tend to pick up on, and their less obvious anatomy (they don't have erections), it's easier for a girl to grow up having completely ignored her own genitals, beyond the demands of urination and menstruation. It's not unheard of for girls to have never masturbated at all by the time they're in college. For a boy, that's far less likely. There is some evidence that connects concordance with other indicators of sexual health. The 2010 meta-analysis done by Chivers and her colleagues suggested that women diagnosed with sexual difficulties had lower concordance, in part because of the way awareness of your own genital response tends to be a turn-on in itself.

If concordance is affected by environment and messaging, however, it may be something we can shift. One way is by masturbating; research shows women who self-pleasure frequently report higher subjective arousal and have higher measures of concordance. But Brotto and Chivers are studying whether concordance levels can also be boosted by, you guessed it ... mindfulness.

A 2016 study published in the *Archives of Sexual Behavior* by Brotto, Chivers and other researchers has shown remarkable results: measures of concordance rise in women with sexual difficulties after just four sessions of mindfulness practice. Using the same device to measure vaginal blood flow, the study showed that women's subjective perception of how aroused they felt matched what their genitals were doing more than it did before they meditated. In contrast, studies that simply asked women to pay more attention to the feelings in their genitals without any meditation instruction did not help. Brotto and Chivers are still not clear on exactly how this works, but it's an absolutely huge finding: women can use mindfulness to boost their 'interoceptive awareness' – their awareness of *what's happening inside their bodies*. (This jives with reports of long-term meditators who say they've become more aware of their breathing, digestion, heartbeat and other internal processes.)

Imagine if our state of mind affected whether a hot iron burned us – whether we could feel it. In sexual experience, this is actually true. If you're distracted from your inner experience, you won't sense sexual sensations as strongly, even if your partner is a cunnilingus virtuoso. Studies have shown that the greater the woman's level of concordance, the more orgasms she tends to report.

Mindfulness also has stress-reduction and relaxation effects that are conducive to enjoying sex, so there could be other benefits at play. A key one is its ethos of non-judgment and acceptance. During one of the group's final silent meditations, Brotto occasionally reads 'The Guest House' by the poet Rumi, a frequent staple of meditation retreats.

> This being human is a guest house.
> Every morning a new arrival.
> A joy, a depression, a meanness,
> some momentary awareness comes
> as an unexpected visitor.
> Welcome and entertain them all, even if they are a crowd of
>   sorrows […]
> They may be clearing you out for some new delight.

Brotto has seen around seven hundred women since her program's inception. At its end, some report having sex with their partners for the first time in years. Others simply report feeling more optimistic about their sexuality, more open to trying different techniques, she says, 'rather than getting into an encounter with hopelessness and the expectation that this is going to fail and a feeling like there's nothing I can do but wait for this to be over.'

With its inclusive, evidence-based language, Brotto's book could be useful not just for women with severe complaints, but for those who simply want to be more fully present with the sex they're already having. She ultimately hopes the techniques trickle down to gynecologists and care providers, so anyone can benefit.

On the surface, these groups of women inching slowly and dutifully through a mindfulness session have little in common with women like my friend Veronica, for whom taking joy in sex is seemingly effortless. Yet both are testing their boundaries in their own ways. They are both experimenting with how much stimulation their nervous systems can take, experiencing their incredible malleability as human beings – whether that is gradually learning how to be okay with sex for the first time or scaling untold heights of ecstasy.

5

Is Pleasure Necessary?

Is the shift toward sexual equality only about fighting for the right to get off – or is it something more?

The bedroom is the last frontier of social justice.
— Drew Deveaux, transgender porn star

This past winter, I found myself having dinner with a table of women I had just met. My partner and I had been staying at a friend's home in Colorado's Vail Valley, surrounded by marijuana retail shops and mountains blanketed in snow so thick it looked like cake icing. It's a relatively progressive part of America. Our hosts had invited their friends, all politically engaged baby boomers with impressive cross-country ski regimens, for a meditation sit and potluck. Over glasses of wine, the conversation drifted from Donald Trump – the Iowa primary was coming up, and the guests, who ranged from solidly Republican to strongly Democrat, were united in horror at him – to what I did for a living.

I gave a potted description of this book, which I was busy finishing. I talked about the idea that sex as it is may not be meeting women's needs, about experimentation among young women and their inspiration by seventies-era feminism. Everyone listened politely, and then there was silence.

'I'm sorry,' said a woman whose politics were the most left-of-centre, 'but isn't all that just kind of, like, First World problems?' Titters rippled around the table. 'I mean, there are people – women – with real problems. Women around the world are suffering from wars, rape, oppression.'

Had I just experienced a boomer-to-millennial sick burn? I felt chastened, redness rising to my throat along with a series of stuttering justifications. Yet part of me was pleased she had said exactly what she thought. It's a perfectly natural reaction. In many ways, nothing could seem more like navel-gazing, more a flagrant demonstration of various varieties of privilege, than the antics in this book. Clit-stroking and naked jerk-off parties? Sure, women's sexuality has been repressed for centuries – but so has every single other aspect of being female. Surely the top priority is not fighting to get women equal orgasms, but achieving pay equity, ending violence against women, securing access to safe abortion, establishing nation-wide childcare, ending discrimination against lesbians, women of colour and trans women, and helping women and girls worldwide who lack basic human rights.

That's all eminently true. Yet the existence of life-and-death needs does not obviate the existence of less dire ones. The right to the pursuit of happiness is more closely linked to other rights than we think. They exist on a continuum of rights. Many of the rights feminists regularly fight for are free-doms *from* – the freedom from violence, harassment, discrimination, unwanted pregnancy, from being cheated out of money earned or a decent education. Sex is more of a freedom *to* – the freedom to live a full life, to experience the body you were born in, to have joy, to soothe life's bitter stings with the sweet honey of the sensuous.

Those sound like nice-to-haves, not need-to-haves, don't they? Yet many of the sex educators I interviewed for this book believe it might be much more than that. Is sex just pleasure, or is it more – is it wellness? Is it an add-on, or does it form part of complete human health? Over and over again, the women in this book gravitated to one phrase, whether they were psychologists, educators or ordinary women explaining why they would brave eight weeks of mindfulness sex therapy: sexual health is about more than just getting off. It's about feeling *whole*. Feeling like every part of you has the right to exist.

'I want to be whole' is what many participants in Lori Brotto's therapy groups say at their first session. 'It's something I hear all the time,' Brotto says.

Here is a conjecture. Men draw from a well of things they take for granted that allow them to stand tall when they enter a room, and one of those things is that having some kind of sexuality is a largely uncontroversial fact of their existence. It's hard to know what the full psychological benefits of this are. What sense of inner strength does it give you to know you can choose to have sex, and – as long as it is consensual and you're not cheating or doing anyone harm – the fact of your having had sex will not be used against you? The mere fact that you like sex, and that other people know it, will not hurt your career, cause people to look askance at you or damage your social standing. It's unlikely your ex will share nude photos of you in order to try to destroy you. For most men, it's the opposite: being a 'stud' will make a guy look *good*. It's something that feels good *and* gives him pride. It gives him mojo and high-fives from friends. If it got out at work, he'd probably get promoted. It's a win-win. His need for sex and his need for success are symbiotic: they dovetail with one another.

This isn't how it is for many women, for whom the fact of being sexual must always be handled carefully, like a national secret: whom you tell must be thought through in detail, lest it make people whisper about you or even destroy your reputation. For this half of humanity, their most natural impulses are at odds with their need to be safe, to thrive and be socially accepted. Even more than half: this is true of anyone we shame or endanger for their sexuality, including women, LGBTQ men and women, and women of colour. We make them choose what half they should be today. When we shame women for being sexual, we force them to divide in two. They must become someone who wants and someone who denies that they want. One part speaks and the other part erases. The double standard boxes women into a place where they have no choice but to lie, to fabulate, to hide their true nature and to learn to do it far too well.

Because of this, they're no longer whole.

Chimamanda Ngozi Adichie said this in her powerful TED Talk, 'We Should All Be Feminists':

> We teach girls shame. Close your legs, cover yourself. We make them feel as though by being born female, they're already guilty of something. And so, girls grow up to be women who cannot see they have desire. They grow up to be women who silence themselves. They grow up to be women who cannot say what they truly think. And they grow up – and this is the worst thing we do to girls – they grow up to be women who have turned pretense into an art form.

How much energy does it take to be your own enemy?

So some women avoid sex. It's not worth it, they say.

It's hard to quantify the sense of infallible confidence that women miss out on because of this. The tall, proud stature that's denied to queer women and intersex women and black women. What if women could get as much of a psychological boost from sex – as much mojo – as men?

Naomi Wolf argues in *Vagina*, inventively and convincingly, that women's creativity and ability to imagine and do daring things in the world can get a huge shot in the arm from sex – and especially from really good sex that includes their pleasure, the kind of sex that leaves them exhausted and smiling beatifically, feeling appreciated and well-fucked. She cites the private letters of artists such as Georgia O'Keeffe and Edith Wharton to show that their highest points of creative achievement were also the times at which they were the most erotically charged, when they were having torrid affairs. The sex helped expand their creativity, she says, and the creativity improved their sex. It was symbiotic.

The judgment that the desire to be sexually whole isn't a big deal or is somehow a distraction from real issues is damaging – it puts the women who have sexual dysfunctions in a true double bind. Women who struggle with low desire, pain during sex and difficulty with arousal suffer twice: once from the feeling that they're broken as women, and a second time because their suffering is invisible. They feel guilty for seeking help. It is not something they can talk about, because their problem is frivolous, despite the fact that the only way to address the problem is to talk about it, to talk and keep talking. (This while countless prime-time television hours are devoted to marketing drugs for men's erectile dysfunction.)

Women and girls benefit from learning all they can about their sexuality. There is a growing trend on North American campuses toward sex education that enshrines affirmative consent. Rather than 'no means no,' it's 'yes means yes.' A 'yes means yes' standard of affirmative consent, according to a law passed in 2014 in California, is an 'affirmative, conscious and voluntary agreement to engage in sexual activity.' Consent must be full-throated and enthusiastic rather than simply the absence of a 'no.' This more stringent standard is moving into some high schools as well college campuses.

This issue has typically been discussed in terms of how it affects the law: how are legal definitions going to catch up with changing social norms? But it also has implications for how schools address sexual pleasure.

If we now expect consent to be based on a woman's desire and volition, then do we need sex ed to better equip women to say 'yes' enthusiastically? Do women have the right to learn about cultivating the positives of sex, not just about preventing the negatives – pregnancy, STD transmission and sexual assault? Yes, because it's hard to expect girls, on campus or anywhere else, to know with clarity and certainty when they want to have sex if they are not encouraged to explore what turns them on in the first place.

In the absence of a clear sense of what feels good, the default for many girls has long been to simply acquiesce to sexual demands from boys because they figure that 'this must be what sex is like.' Knowing the possibilities that sex holds, learning what you're attracted to and what kind of touch, pressure and stimulation feel good, is a key tool in helping to know when touch feels wrong, too hard, too fast or painful. Without encouragement to experiment with self-pleasure, to fantasize and to develop clear preferences early on (i.e., in their preteens), it's much harder for women to give that full-throated *Yes, this is what I want* in their first sexual encounters – the consent that legislators now say participants in a sexual situation must wait for. As feminist philosopher Luce Irigaray wrote in her meditation on love, *To Be Two*, yes and no must emerge not in isolation but in *relationship* with one another.

In a vacuum created by poor or nonexistent sex ed and the reluctance of parents to talk to girls about anything beyond avoiding pregnancy and sexual assault, however, young women are turning to the internet for sex ed. That's not working out so well.

'We got an entry from a girl who was thirteen and she said, "I'm so scared to have sex, I'm crying almost every night because I saw a video of sex on a boy's phone at school and I didn't realise that when you have sex a woman has to be hurting and crying."' That's Laura Bates, founder of the Everyday Sexism Project, in an interview this year with the *Independent* newspaper in the U.K. Her blog receives submissions from women about discrimination, sexism and harassment they experience, and this teen was assaulted by the media her friends consumed and that surrounded her. Her own budding sexuality was quashed.

Porn gives boys and girls a twisted version of how sex works, where choking, slapping and coercion are common. Hugging, caressing, full-body massage, foreplay, clitoral stroking and cunnilingus that lasts long enough to produce an orgasm are not. Another act common in porn is anal sex. A sexual behaviour survey conducted by the Center for Sexual Health Promotion at Indiana University showed that 70 percent of women say sexual encounters involving anal are painful. Although anal can feel good for both partners if it's done slowly and safely, with a lot of communication and even more lube, that information isn't found in a wank video. One of the tricks employed in porn is to 'hide' lube inside a performer's vagina or anus off-camera, so that it doesn't interrupt the action or look 'staged' men don't want to be reminded that they're watching a performance. So videos tend to show rough sex as if it requires no lube. In the case of anal, too little lube can result in tearing and bleeding. Yet many women are blamed by their partners if they don't enjoy it or 'relax' into it. If porn stars seem to love it, why can't they?

A British survey of college students showed 60 percent consult porn in part for information on how sex works, according to Peggy Orenstein, whose 2016 book *Girls and Sex: Navigating the Complicated New Landscape* bravely calls for greater openness in American culture about the messages and facts we give young girls about sex. The answer is not a war on porn, she says, which wouldn't work anyway, but balancing it with more explicit information from trusted sources. She movingly makes the case for a greater emphasis in sex ed on female pleasure and self-knowledge (not to mention same-sex relationships, which are also marginalized). Too many programs tend to address erections as a central topic while featuring diagrams of women that don't even show the clitoris. Boys have sex drives; girls have babies. Better education is needed. A 2005 study of undergraduate students led by Lisa

D. Wade at Occidental College found that for information on where the clitoris was, women rarely consulted the most reliable source of knowledge – their own bodies – and undergrads of both genders saw women's pleasure as incidental to that of men.

It may be hard to believe that girls really need more information in an age when they talk about sex openly and hang out on Tinder. But comfort with sex does not necessarily mean comfort with one's own pleasure.

One recent summer, I met a young woman at a lunch hangout in a friend's backyard. She was brassy, outgoing and opinionated. When I told her about the book I was writing, she revealed that in addition to pursuing an accounting degree, she sold sex. She agreed to let me interview her anonymously. We met on the back patio of a coffee shop in Toronto's Cabbagetown neighbourhood a few weeks later, and she told me about her work and life. She was smart, funny and self-sufficient. She also seemed like the most sexually relaxed person on planet earth. In the middle of our talk, she got a call – a client wanted an appointment with her in an hour. 'I have to go get a glass of water,' she said breezily, and returned with a big pint glass that she began to drink. This guy's thing was pissing, she explained, so she had to make sure her bladder would be full enough to pee all over him.

Despite her laid-back attitude, one sex act made her feel guilty: masturbating. The genitals of her clients didn't bother her, but her own seemed 'gross.' She rarely felt much during sex and rarely had an orgasm. She sometimes faked it for clients, who expect her to come.

Lest you conclude that unhealthy attitudes toward your body are the inevitable consequence of doing sex work, I present to you, once again, Robyn Red.

Red is a Toronto sex worker of a different sort, also in her early thirties. She also agreed to meet me for coffee one sunny day last year, wearing a long, comfy skirt and Doc Martens. Originally from North Bay, Ontario, she had been studying English lit and queer theory at Western University when she started escorting for extra money right before defending her Master's thesis. She was apprehensive at first, she said, but approached it as an academic – by doing research. Once she found an agency she liked, she began to see clients for roughly $300 per hour. 'It wasn't the fantasy where you're going out to the opera,' she smiles, but it was okay. What she started to notice was that some clients wanted more than sex – they wanted sympathy.

'I've always been that kind of person – I sit down at a bar and people talk to me,' she says. 'Some people see therapists. Some people see escorts.' There was a man who told her he'd been sexually abused; another had problems with his father. There was something about the vulnerability of sex that seemed to be helping them process their emotions.

In 2011, Red began designing a new type of business, quitting the agency and working for herself. She offers erotic and therapeutic massage to both women and men. Some clients see her every week. The sexual release is part of a larger therapeutic release, where clients work to shed 'self-limiting beliefs' and confront major life changes. 'I use my body to read their bodies,' she says. She hesitates to describe what she does as tantric, a term she derides as 'culturally appropriative,' but women who see her do tend to have extended orgasms. 'It just happens!' she laughs.

I don't think Marvin Gaye would have objected to calling this kind of work 'sexual healing.' She says her job hasn't had ill effects on her own sex life or happiness in relationships. Her work is particularly sought after by other sex workers, she says, who come to her to work on emotional issues that come up in the course of their jobs.

I don't mean to set up a dichotomy between 'bad' and 'good' kinds of sex work. There is nothing wrong with any kind of sex work, as long as it is freely chosen and workers have rights. And it's important to note that the ability to have a 'respectable' sex work practice with elevated, holistic overtones isn't equally available to all sex workers of all racial and class backgrounds, immigration statuses and gender identities – it's partly a function of white, cis privilege.

I'm describing Red's innovative practice simply to offer a glimpse into a future world where sex is destigmatized and seen as an integral part of health. Where sex work is just a kind of body work. Where people who are lonely and crave touch need not feel shame for it. Where sexual healing is available to people who are not in love. Red says her clients are asking for it.

Integrative health educator and dance teacher Anita Boeninger believes moving outside conventional sex could help heal not just individuals, but our goal-driven culture as a whole.

The founder of New York City's SOMA Wellness Arts and women's leadership group the Embodied Femme, she teaches a variety of workshops to help women find their inner goddess, and topics include sensual movement and voice training. She shakes her head at the notion that a pill could ever be the right technology for women's desire or pleasure.

'It's so classic,' she says. 'Let's reduce everything to its parts! Just rub that button and it'll work better now!' Women experience sex as a holistic part of life rather than an act or set of acts – it's why they feel inexplicably horny for a day or for a year, and then suddenly, not so much. It's connected to other things happening in their lives, including stress. Our lives have become so multi-tasked and overworked, she says, that in some ways, sexual dysfunction is a canary in the coal mine.

'A lot of the time nothing's "wrong" with women that they can't orgasm,' says Boeninger. 'It's just tension. It's no wonder we can't let go. Sex is not about the act in the moment. It's how you live your life. If you live a high-stress, high-intensity lifestyle, your lovemaking can't switch up.

'Sex is all of life – it's life as the lover,' she says. 'It's not an act. It's a realm. It's a space. It's a state. I think that's what a more feminine culture can bring back into this culture.'

At its deepest, this push from so many women to transform their sexuality has something in common with other holistic trends, including yoga, slow food and holistic medicine. It is yet another attempt to part ways – at least for the length of time it takes to lose yourself – with a driven, distracted, isolated and hyper-stimulated way of living today that no one seems to consciously choose, but that chooses us. For some, it's an attempt to loosen 'the mooring ropes' that tie us to a limited self, to briefly become more than we are. The fact that sexuality resists attempts to be simplified should be a wake-up call.

Sex is much more mysterious and meaningful than we pretend it is. The mystery is one of its best parts. Why paint sex as a thin caricature of what it truly is – a way to know ourselves at the deepest level?

As I said early on, this little book is meant as a provocation, a poke, food for further thought. It is descriptive rather than prescriptive. It's not a list of things people should necessarily run out and do. Women shouldn't feel the need to look for a local yoni steam or orgasmic meditation meeting. These experiments aren't for everyone! It is simply, I hope, a look at the way an aspect of the world that we often take for granted is changing right under our noses.

It is meant as an objection to the idea that there is one way of being sexual – or at least, one 'normal' way. Sexuality is about individual expression: there are as many ways to be sexual as there are ways to be a woman. There are so many aspects of this discussion I barely touched on: the diverse sexual experiences of women of size, disabled women, women who have given birth, menopausal women, elderly women, genderqueer and intersex women – women whose experiences are regularly erased when sex is brought up. There's the asexuality movement, which is gaining momentum, encouraging people to be proud of the choice to explore celibacy. It's all in service of feeling more comfortable in our own skin. Until we make contact with some sexually evolved alien civilization (which might create more problems than it solves), *homo sapiens* remains the sole living organism with the potential to experience high levels of joy, bliss and deep fulfillment from reproduction.

'The all-consuming ecstasy of the human orgasm took three billion years of evolution to appear,' writes science journalist Zoe Cormier. 'It is a gift.' The catch is that because of the peculiarity of being human, the joy of sex is a biological gift that is as easy to snatch away as it is to bestow. It is a perk of nature, but it thrives on the best impulses of culture – compassion, intelligence, acceptance and imagination.

Notes

1. This isn't to say all porn is misogynist. There is porn made by women, and producers that mandate on-set STD safety and fair wages for performers. But they're in the minority. Most porn degrades women and girls – and almost all of it degrades sex. The great swath of average, mainstream porn Gavrieli accurately describes as 'sex without hands': unrealistic fucking in which the only body parts that touch are the genitals, because caressing and embracing would get in the way of the camera's lens.

2. For an excellent look at contemporary sexuality in the Middle East, read Canadian-Egyptian journalist Shereen El Feki's *Sex and the Citadel: Intimate Life in a Changing Arab World* (Anchor, 2014).

3. Quoted in Shereen El Feki's *Sex and the Citadel*.

4. Quoted in David Gordon White, *Kiss of the Yogini: 'Tantric Sex' in its South Asian Contexts* (University of Chicago Press, 2006).

5. In 2001, the Federative Committee on Anatomical Terminology accepted 'female prostate' as an accurate term for the Skene's gland. The word has not passed into common parlance.

6. Carroll Smith-Rosenberg and Charles Rosenberg, 'The Female Animal: Medical and Biological Views of Woman and Her Role in Nineteenth Century America,' *Journal of American History* 60 (1973).

7. Betty Dodson, *Sex for One: The Joy of Selfloving* (Harmony, 1986). Dodson writes: 'It was clear that masturbation as a ritual created harmony between my body and mind the same way that meditation did. After having an orgasm, or after meditating, I was always more peaceful, centered in my body, and relaxed in my mind.'

8. A strain of 1970s French feminist theory, *écriture feminine* held that language itself was male in its very structure and had to be reimagined and reinvented by women.

9. As I mentioned earlier, this analysis only covers trends I've observed among women in Western, democratic societies, especially North America. But many fascinating forms of rebellion, self-expression and experimentation are emerging right now among women in cultures

around the world.

10. Latin for 'under the rose,' *sub rosa* refers to activities done in secret. It comes from Aphrodite, the goddess of fertility and love, who gave a rose to her son, Eros, to bribe Harpocrates, the god of silence, to keep mum about her sexual liaisons.

11. Native American leaders have heavily criticized Reagan and others in the group for this claim, arguing some of its terminology has no origin in any Aboriginal language and that there are no spiritual sexual teachings in Cherokee culture. This is made all the knottier by the fact that, since Reagan's death, most of Quodoushka's teachers have been white Americans and Canadians. Barbara Brachi, who teaches a Quodoushka class at Toronto's Institute of Contemporary Shamanic Studies, says she has welcomed members of the First Nations community to drop in and observe her teaching, and they have. 'They have the right to do that,' she says. 'The main thing they're looking for is, is there sincerity and is there truth here? Are the people here honouring the spirit in the correct way?'

12. I was at a women's potluck hangout last year, and I was describing this experiment when a friend tapped me on the shoulder. 'I was one of her subjects for that study!' she said proudly. My friend promptly sketched me a colourful picture of herself sitting in the famous easy chair, her ladybusiness hooked up to the device.

Works Cited

American Psychiatric Association. *Diagnostic and Statistical Manual of Mental Disorders: DSM-5*. Arlington, VA: American Psychiatric Publishing, 2013.

Bataille, Georges. *Madame Edwarda*. trans. Austryn Wainhouse. London: Marion Boyars, 1989.

Bergner, Daniel. 'What Do Women Want?' *New York Times Magazine*, January 22, 2009.

———. *What Do Women Want? Adventures in the Science of Female Desire*. New York: Ecco, 2013.

Breslaw, Anna, Marina Khidekel and Michelle Ruiz. 'Cosmo's Female Orgasm Survey.' *Cosmopolitan*, March 16, 2015.

Brotto, Lori A., Meredith L. Chivers, et al. 'Mindfulness-Based Sex Therapy Improves Genital-Subjective Arousal Concordance in Women with Sexual Desire/Arousal Difficulties.' *Archives of Sexual Behavior* (2016) (forthcoming)

Carmichael, Marie S. et al. 'Relationships Among Cardiovascular, Muscular, and Oxytocin Responses During Human Sexual Activity.' *Archives of Sexual Behavior* 23, no. 1 (1994).

Charles, Amara. *The Sexual Practices of Quodoushka: Teachings from the Nagual Tradition*. Rochester: Destiny, 2011.

Carvalheira, Ana A. et al. 'Dropout in the Treatment of Erectile Dysfunction with PDE5: A Study o n Predictors and a Qualitative Analysis of Reasons for Discontinuation.' *The Journal of Sexual Medicine* 9, no. 9 (2012).

Chivers, Meredith L. , M. C. Seto et al. 'Gender and Sexual Orientation Differences in Sexual Response to Sexual Activities Versus Gender of Actors in Sexual Films.' *Journal of Personality and Social Psychology* 93, no. 6 (2007).

———. 'Agreement of Genital and Subjective Measures of Sexual Arousal in Men and Women: A Meta-analysis.' *Archives of Sexual Behavior* 39, no. 1 (2010).

Clément, Catherine. *Syncope: The Philosophy of Rapture*. Minneapolis: University of Minnesota Press, 1994.

Cohen, H. D., Rosen, R. C. and Goldstein, L. 'Electroencephalographic Laterality Changes during Human Sexual Orgasm.' Archives of Sexual Behavior 5, no. 3 (1976). Colombo, Realdo, quoted in Thomas Laqueur, *Making Sex: Body and Gender from the Greeks to Freud*. Cambridge, MA: Harvard, 1992.

Cormier, Zoe. *Sex, Drugs and Rock 'n' Roll: The Science of Hedonism and the Hedonism of Science*. London: Profile Books, 2014.

Davies, Anna. 'Why Do Women Still Fake It?,' *Elle*, December 2014.

Diamond, Lisa M. *Sexual Fluidity: Understanding Women's Love and Desire*. Cambridge, MA: Harvard, 2008.

Dickson, E. J. 'These Real Women Want to Show You How to Give Them an Orgasm.' *Mic*, December 22, 2015.

Dodson, Betty. *Sex for One: The Joy of Selfloving*. New York: Crown Trade Paperbacks, 1974.

Evans, Dayna. 'Meet the Woman Who Started a Blog About Female Orgasms.' *New York*, September 2, 2015.

El Feki, Shereen. *Sex and the Citadel: Intimate Life in a Changing Arab World*. Toronto: Doubleday, 2013.

Garcia, J. R., S. G. Massey, A. M. Merriwether and S. M. Seibold-Simpson. 'Orgasm Experience Among Emerging Adult Men and Women: Relationship Context and Attitudes toward Uncommitted Sex.' (Paper presented at the annual convention of the Association for Psychological Science, Washington, DC, May 26, 2013)

Garcia, J. R., Lloyd, E. A., Wallen, K., and Fisher, H. E. 'Variation in Orgasm Occurrence by Sexual Orientation in a Sample of U.S. Singles,' *Journal of Sexual Medicine* 11, no. 11 (2014).

Gittes, R. F., and Nakamura, R. M. 'Female Urethral Syndrome: A Female Prostatitis?' *Western Journal of Medicine* 164, no. 5 (1996).

Heart, Mikaya. *When the Earth Moves: Women and Orgasm*. Berkeley, CA: Celestial Arts, 1998.

Hillman, David and Carla Mazzio, eds., *The Body in Parts: Fantasies of Corporeality in Early Modern Europe*. New York: Routledge, 1997.

Irigaray, Luce. *To Be Two*. New York: Routledge, 2001.

Jannini, Emmanuele A., et al. 'Beyond the G-spot: Clitourethrovaginal Complex Anatomy in Female Orgasm,' *Nature Reviews Urology* 11 (2014).

Jansen, Carlyle. *Sex Yourself: The Woman's Guide to Mastering Masturbation and Achieving Powerful Orgasms*. Beverly, MA: Quiver, 2015.

Kerner, Ian. *She Comes First: The Thinking Man's Guide to Pleasuring a Woman*. New York: HarperCollins, 2004.

Kobelt, Georg Ludwig. *The Male and Female Organs of Sexual Arousal in Man and Some Other Mammals*. 1844.

Komisaruk, Barry R., Carlos Beyer-Flores and Beverly Whipple. *The Science of Orgasm*. Baltimore: Johns Hopkins University Press, 2006.

Lacan, Jacques. *Encore*. Paris: Editions du Seuil, 1998.

Lydon, Susan. 'The Politics of Orgasm,' in Robin Morgan, ed., *Sisterhood Is Powerful: An Anthology of Writings From the Women's Liberation Movement*. New York: Random House, 1970.

Meston, C. M., Levin, R. J., Sipski, M. L., Hull, E. M., and Heiman, J. R. 'Women's Orgasm.' *Annual Review of Sex Research* 15, no. 1 (2004).

Meston, Cindy and David Buss. *Why Women Have Sex: Understanding Sexual Motivations from Adventure to Revenge (and Everything in Between)*. New York: Times Books, 2009.

Money, J., G. Wainwright, and D. Hingburger. *The Breathless Orgasm*. New York: Prometheus, 1991.

Moon, Allison and k. d. diamond. *Girl Sex 101*. La Vergne, TN: Lightning Source, 2015.

Nagoski, Emily. *Come As You Are: The Surprising New Science that Will Transform Your Sex Life*. New York: Simon & Schuster, 2015.

O'Connell, Helen E. et al. 'Anatomy of the Clitoris.' *Journal of Urology* 174 (2005).

Orenstein, Peggy. *Girls and Sex: Navigating the Complicated New Landscape*. New York: HarperCollins, 2016.

Peplau, Letitia Anne, and Linda D. Garnets. 'A New Paradigm for Understanding Women's Sexuality and Sexual Orientation.' *Journal of Social Issues* 56, no. 2 (2000).

Reid, Daniel P. *The Tao of Health, Sex and Longevity: A Modern Practical Guide to the Ancient Way*. New York: Fireside, 1989.

Roach, Mary. *Bonk: The Curious Coupling of Science and Sex*. New York: W. W. Norton & Co., 2008.

Rosner, Fred J., and David Bleich, eds. *Jewish Bioethics*. New York: Sanhedrin, 1979.

Salama, Samuel, et al. 'Nature and Origin of "Squirting" in Female Sexuality.' *The Journal of Sexual Medicine* 12, no. 3 (2015).

Sales, Nancy Jo. 'Tinder and the Dawn of the "Dating Apocalypse."' *Vanity Fair*, August 2015.

Smith-Rosenberg, Carroll and Charles Rosenberg. 'The Female Animal: Medical and Biological Views of Woman and Her Role in Nineteenth Century America.' *Journal of American History* 60 (1973).

J. Walter Thompson Intelligence. 'Study of Youth Attitudes toward Gender.' New York: J. Walter Thompson Group, 2016.

Traister, Rebecca. 'The Game is Rigged.' *New York*, Oct. 20, 2015.

Vance, Ellen Belle and Nathaniel N. Wagner. 'Written Descriptions of Orgasm: A Study of Sex Differences.' *Archives of Sexual Behavior* 5, no. 1 (1976).

White, David Gordon. *Kiss of the Yogini: 'Tantric Sex' in its South Asian Contexts*. Chicago: University of Chicago, 2003.

Wade, Lisa D. et al. 'The Incidental Orgasm: The Presence of Clitoral Knowledge and the Absence of Orgasm for Women.' *Women & Health* 42, no. 1 (2005).

Wolf, Naomi. *Vagina: A New Biography*. New York: Ecco, 2012.

Suggested Reading

Informative books about sex tailored to women

Come As You Are: The Surprising New Science That Will Transform Your Sex Life, by Emily Nagoski, Ph.D.
If you only buy one book from this list, make it this one. Practical and revolutionary at the same time.

Girl Sex 101, by Allison Moon and K. D. Diamond
An inclusive guide with specific information for LGBTIQ readers.

Sex Yourself: The Woman's Guide to Mastering Masturbation and Achieving Powerful Orgasms, by Carlyle Jansen
Practical tips for having bigger orgasms by yourself.

Sex For One: The Joy of Selfloving, by Betty Dodson, Ph.D.
The classic book about loving yourself from the queen of masturbation.

Becoming Orgasmic: A Sexual and Personal Growth Program for Women, by Julia R.Heiman, Ph.D. and Joseph LoPiccolo, Ph.D.
Ideal for women who wish to have their first orgasm, or for whom climax is difficult.

Women's Anatomy of Arousal, by Sheri Winston
Tons of information on sex and the female body.

The Illustrated Guide to Extended Massive Orgasm, by Steve and Vera Bodansky, Ph.Ds
For those who wish to take their orgasms further.

Slow Sex: The Art and Craft of the Female Orgasm, by Nicole Daedone
For those curious about orgasmic meditation.

Acknowledgements

Thank you, first of all, to my initial editor on this project, Jason McBride, and Coach House editorial director Alana Wilcox, whose willingness to let a young journalist attempt a book based on a few vague hunches was unexpected and generous. Thank you to Beverly and Phil, who kindly lent out their Colorado home as a much-needed writing retreat, and Ted and Susan, whose cottage was home to many long writing days. Thank you to Vanessa, who trusted me with a very intimate story. Profound thanks to the Ontario Arts Council for their generous Works in Progress grant, which helped me to complete this book.

Many smart people made great suggestions, lent me books, answered onslaughts of weird questions, introduced me to subjects, offered moral support and generally showed up at magically perfect junctures to say or do helpful things. I'm no doubt missing some names here, so my apologies in advance for leaving anyone out: David Hayes, Christina Berkely, Marni Jackson, Zoe Cormier, Desmond Cole, Lori Brotto, Barry Komisaruk, Lucy Becker, Carlyle Jansen, Tobi Hill-Meyer, Jeet Heer, Lisa Zimmerman, Eric Holt, Julia Rosenberg, Lisan Jutras, Kelli Korducki, Tasha Schumann, Andréa Cohen-B. and all the talented ladies who appeared in the book trailer.

Thank you to my mom, Cheryl, for teaching me the alphabet and always supporting the writing that emerged as a consequence, even if you weren't always sure what the hell it was about. Thank you to my dad, Jack, for your support for and tolerance of my antics. Thank you to my high school teacher Lewis Fried for your kindness and encouragement.

Most of all, thank you to my friend, co-adventurer, vulva illustrator and fiancé Jeff Warren, without whom this book would never have existed at all. Your loving support and unwavering ability to discuss ideas, listen to strange sex facts and offer wise and irreplaceable feedback make me the luckiest, happiest lady in the land.

About the Author

Sarah Barmak is a Toronto free-lance journalist and author. Her writing has appeared in *Maclean's*, the *Globe and Mail*, the *Toronto Star*, *Canadian Business*, *Marketing* and *Reader's Digest*.

About the
Exploded Views Series

Exploded Views is a series of probing, provocative essays that offer surprising perspectives on the most intriguing cultural issues and figures of our day. Longer than a typical magazine article but shorter than a full-length book, these are punchy salvos written by some of North America's most lyrical journalists and critics. Spanning a variety of forms and genres – history, biography, polemic, commentary – and published simultaneously in all digital formats and handsome, collectible print editions, this is literary reportage that at once investigates, illuminates and intervenes.

www.chbooks.com/explodedviews

Typeset in Goodchild Pro and Gibson Pro. Goodchild was designed by Nick Shinn in 2002 at his ShinnType foundry in Orangeville, Ontario. Shinn's design takes its inspiration from French printer Nicholas Jenson who, at the height of the Renaissance in Venice, used the basic Carolingian minuscule calligraphic hand and classic roman inscriptional capitals to arrive at a typeface that produced a clear and even texture that most literate Europeans could read. Shinn's design captures the calligraphic feel of Jensen's early types in a more refined digital format. Gibson was designed by Rod McDonald in honour of John Gibson FGDC (1928–2011), Rod's long-time friend and one of the founders of the Society of Graphic Designers of Canada. It was McDonald's intention to design a solid, contemporary and affordable sans serif face.

Printed at the old Coach House on bpNichol Lane in Toronto, Ontario, on Rolland Opaque Natural paper, which was manufactured, acid-free, in Saint-Jérôme, Quebec, from 50 percent recycled paper, and it was printed with vegetable-based ink on a 1965 Heidelberg KORD offset litho press. Its pages were folded on a Baumfolder, gathered by hand, bound on a Sulby Auto-Minabinda and trimmed on a Polar single-knife cutter.

Edited by Heidi Waechtler and Alana Wilcox
Copy edited by Stuart Ross
Series cover design by Ingrid Paulson
Cover embroidery by Shannon Gerard (shannongerard.org), photographed
    by Lauren Perruzza
Author photo by Kayla Rocca Photography

Coach House Books
80 bpNichol Lane
Toronto ON M5S 3J4
Canada

416 979 2217
800 367 6360

mail@chbooks.com
www.chbooks.com